CW01468264

CGP

11+ Practice Paper

For Ages 9-10

Set B: Paper 2

For the CEM Test

Read the following:

Do not open this booklet or start the test until you are told to do so.

1. This test can be taken in either multiple-choice or write-in format.

2. If you are taking it as a multiple-choice test, you should mark your answer to each question in pencil on the separate answer sheet. Mark the correct box quickly and neatly using a horizontal line.

3. If you are taking it as a write-in test, you should write your answer to each question in pencil on the paper. Write your answer carefully in the space provided or, if there is a range of options, mark the correct box quickly and neatly using a horizontal line.

4. If you make a mistake, rub it out and mark your new answer clearly.

5. There are three sections in this test.

6. The time allowed for each section is given at the start of that section. You will have a total of 45 minutes to complete the timed sections of the test.

7. Each section includes examples showing you how to answer the questions. You may refer to these examples at any time as you work through the section.

8. Do as many questions as you can. For some questions you will be given a range of options — if you get stuck on one of these questions, choose the answer that you think is most likely to be correct, then move on to the next question. If you get stuck on a question for which no options are given, leave it and move on to the next question. If you have time at the end of the section, go back and have another go at the questions you could not answer.

9. You should do any rough working on a separate piece of paper.

Work carefully, but go as quickly as you can.

© CGP 2019

Section 1: Verbal Reasoning — Odd One Out

Example   Read this example question. You may return to this example at any time as you work through this section.

Three of the words in each list are linked.
Mark the rectangle under the word that is **not** related to these three.

A   sister   brother   family   cousin
☐   ☐   ▬   ☐

⚠️ **Wait until you are told to go on** ⚠️

🕐 **You have 4 minutes to complete this section** 🕐

There are 12 questions in this section

Three of the words in each list are linked.
Mark the rectangle under the word that is **not** related to these three.

1   melon   pineapple   mango   carrot
☐   ☐   ☐   ☐

2   workbook   notepad   whiteboard   diary
☐   ☐   ☐   ☐

3   draw   tie   connection   stalemate
☐   ☐   ☐   ☐

4   scrubbed   swept   mopped   duster
☐   ☐   ☐   ☐

5   hexagon   triangle   pentagon   sphere
☐   ☐   ☐   ☐

6   vulture   elephant   giraffe   baboon
☐   ☐   ☐   ☐

7   astray   route   lost   adrift
□   □   □   □

8   loud   boom   splat   bang
□   □   □   □

9   wordsearch   hangman   hopscotch   crossword
□   □   □   □

10   weld   bind   mixture   combine
□   □   □   □

11   cake   crumble   jelly   brownie
□   □   □   □

12   spotless   flawless   invisible   unmarked
□   □   □   □

✖ Stop — you may check your answers in this section only

Section 2: Non-Verbal Reasoning

Example Read these example questions. You may return to these examples at any time as you work through this section.

A Look at how the first two figures are changed, and then work out which option would look like the third figure if you changed it in the same way:

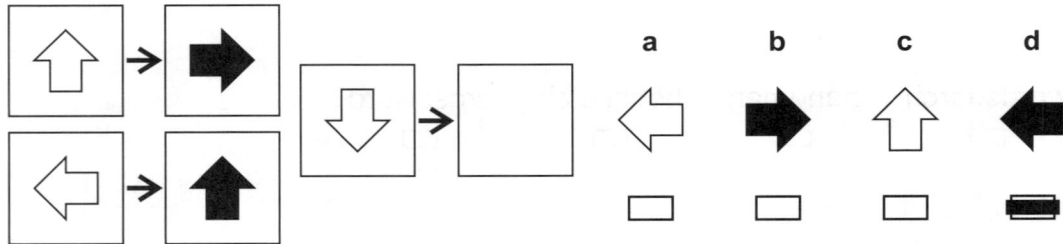

B Work out which of the four hexagons on the right best fits in place of the missing hexagon in the grid:

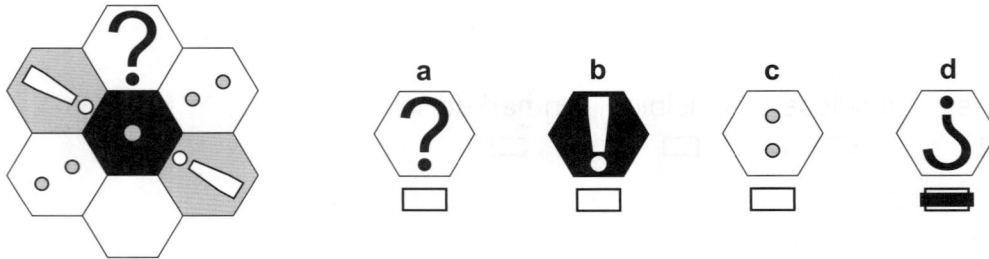

C Work out which option would look like the figure on the left if it was rotated:

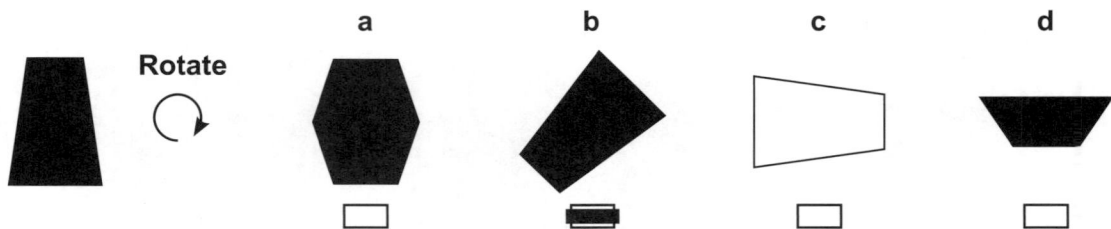

Rotate

⚠️ **Wait until you are told to go on** ⚠️

There are 18 questions in this section

Look at how the first two figures are changed, and then work out which option would look like the third figure if you changed it in the same way:

①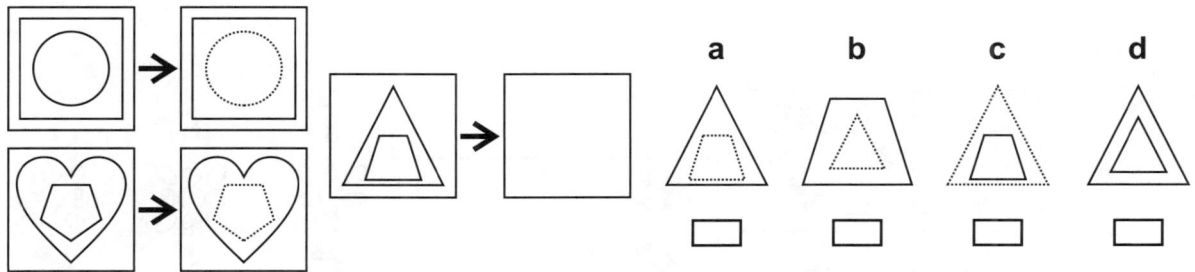

②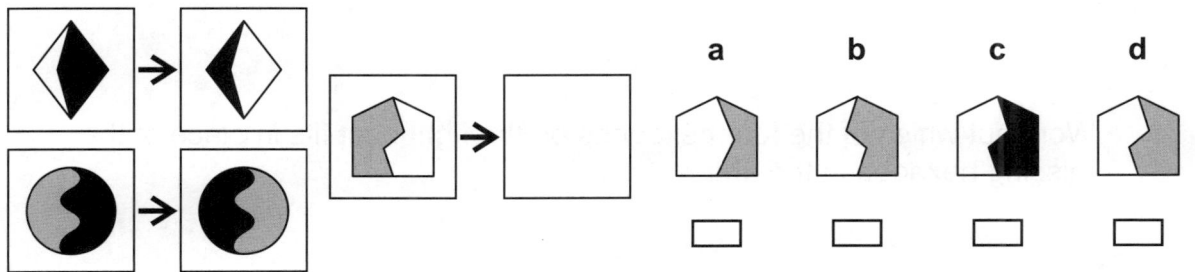

③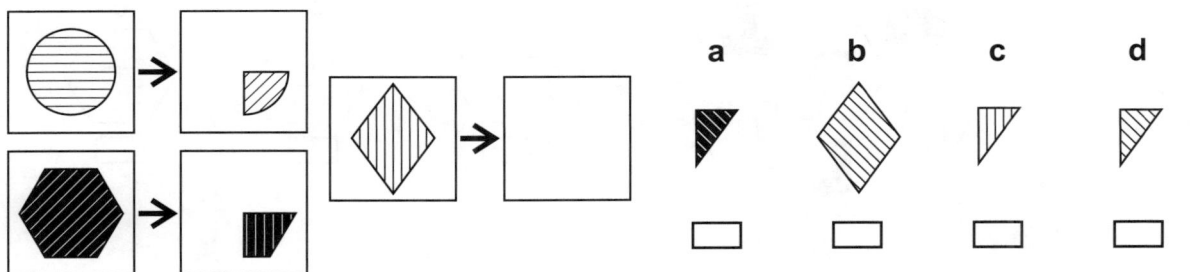

④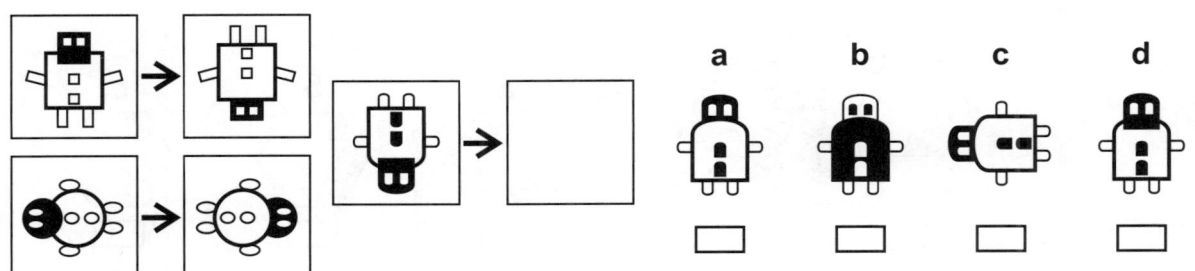

Go to the next question ⇨

(5)

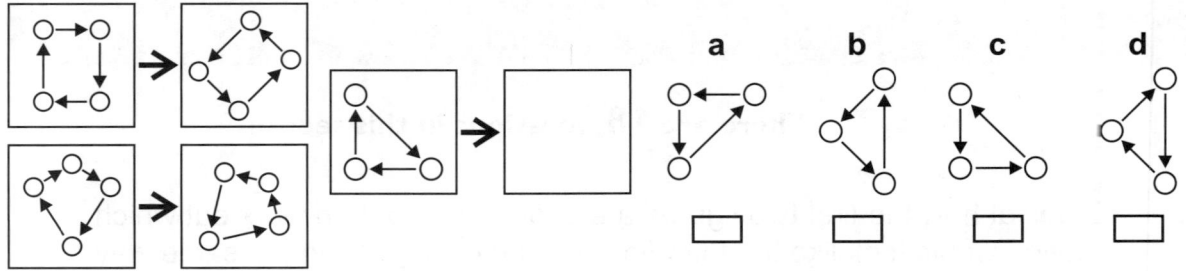

	a	b	c	d
	□	□	□	□

(6)

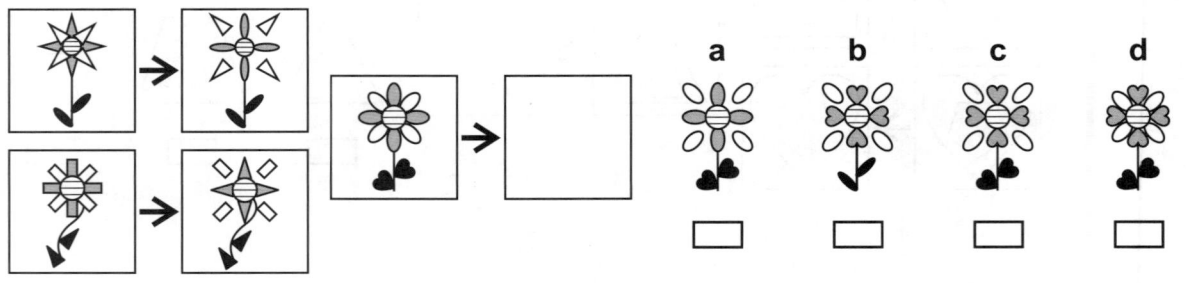

	a	b	c	d
	□	□	□	□

Work out which of the four hexagons on the right best fits in place of the missing hexagon in the grid:

(7)

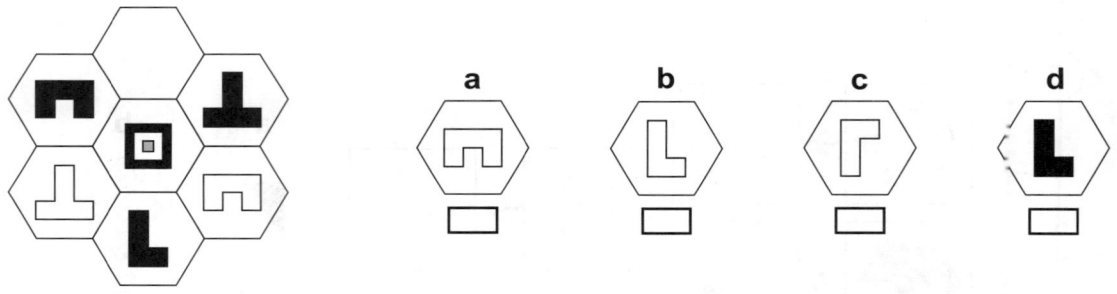

(8)

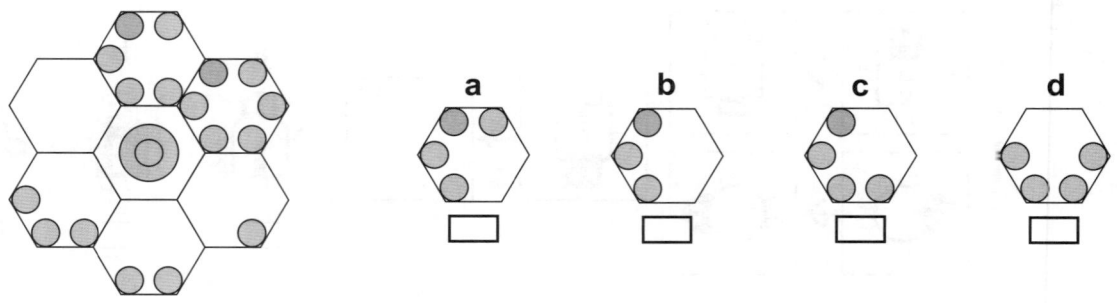

9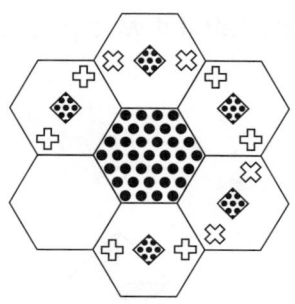

a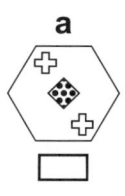

b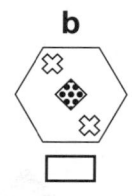

c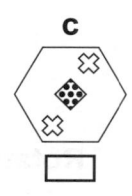

d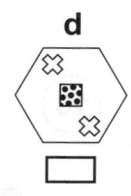

10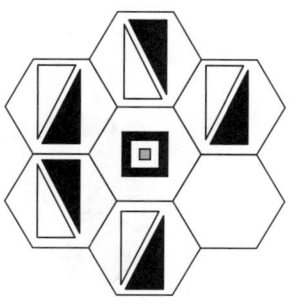

a

b

c

d

11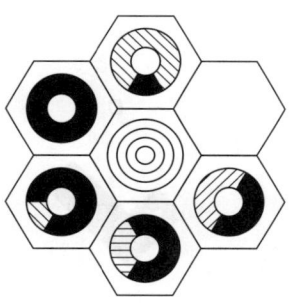

a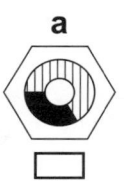

b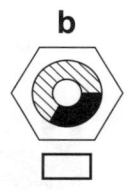

c

d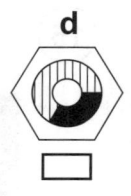

12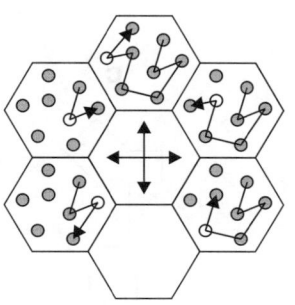

a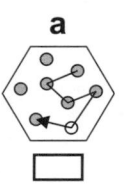

b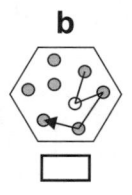

c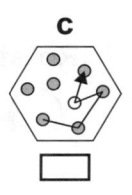

d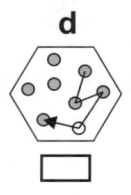

Go to the next question ⇨

Work out which option would look like the figure on the left if it was rotated:

(13)   **Rotate**

a   b   c   d

☐   ☐   ☐   ☐

(14)   **Rotate**

a   b   c   d

☐   ☐   ☐   ☐

(15)   **Rotate**

a   b   c   d

☐   ☐   ☐   ☐

(16)   **Rotate**

a   b   c   d

☐   ☐   ☐   ☐

17 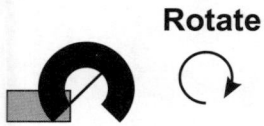 **Rotate**

a

b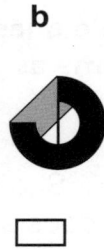

c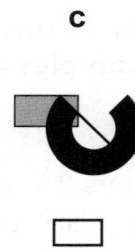

d

☐   ☐   ☐   ☐

18 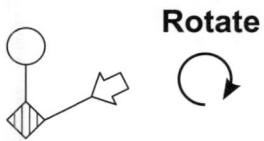 **Rotate**

a

b

c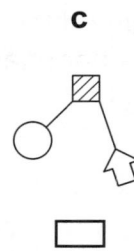

d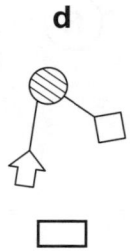

☐   ☐   ☐   ☐

⊗ **Stop — you may check your answers in this section only**

9

© CGP 2019

Example   Read these example questions. You may return to these examples at any time as you work through this section.

(A)   Barbara buys 2 litres of milk. She drinks 250 ml of the milk.
How many millilitres of milk does she have left?

$\boxed{1}\boxed{7}\boxed{5}\boxed{0}$ ml

(B)   Dustin counted the number of guests staying at his hotel over five months.
He made a bar chart of his results.

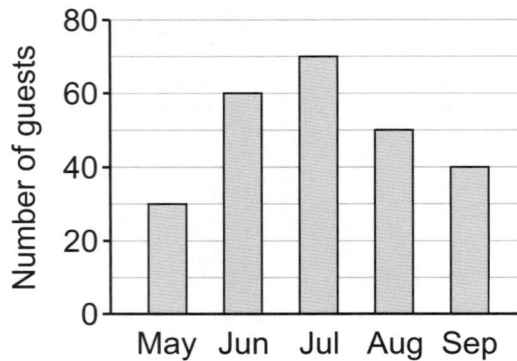

(B1)   How many guests were there in total over the five months?

$\boxed{}\boxed{2}\boxed{5}\boxed{0}$

(B2)   How many more guests stayed in June than stayed in May?

$\boxed{3}\boxed{0}$

(B3)   What fraction of the guests stayed in August?

$\frac{1}{25}$	$\frac{1}{5}$	$\frac{7}{25}$	$\frac{1}{50}$	$\frac{2}{5}$
☐	▬	☐	☐	☐

⚠️ **Wait until you are told to go on** ⚠️

This section contains single-part and multi-part questions.

There are **25** questions in this section

1   Fill in the missing number to make this calculation correct.

32 + ⬚⬚ = 80

2   Jonah is making jam. The amount of sugar needed to make one batch of jam is shown on the scales below.

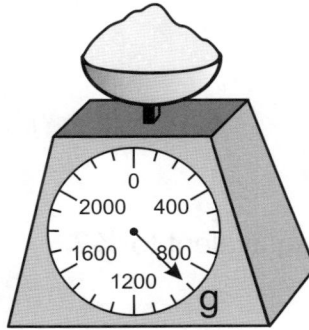

How much sugar would Jonah need to make two batches of jam?

⬚⬚⬚⬚⬚ g

3   Which one of these triangles would go in the shaded part of the sorting table?

☐ scalene

☐ isosceles

☐ equilateral

☐ right-angled

	Three equal sides	Fewer than three equal sides
May contain an obtuse angle		
Cannot contain an obtuse angle		

Go to the next question ⟹

(4) Shape X is reflected in the mirror line shown.
Which of the shapes below is the reflection of shape X?

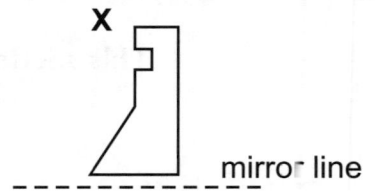

X

mirror line

A   B   C   D   E

A   B   C   D   E
☐   ☐   ☐   ☐   ☐

(5) Which of these fractions is equivalent to $\frac{3}{5}$?

$\frac{3}{15}$ $\frac{12}{20}$ $\frac{5}{10}$ $\frac{4}{6}$ $\frac{6}{9}$
☐   ☐   ☐   ☐   ☐

(6) The maximum distance a type of aeroplane can fly in one trip is 8820 miles, to the nearest 10 miles. Which of these could be the actual distance the plane can fly?

8919 miles   8830 miles   8721 miles   8815 miles   8829 miles
☐   ☐   ☐   ☐   ☐

(7) A carnival is held on the last Saturday in July every year.
In 2018, 19th July was a Thursday.

a) What was the date of the carnival in 2018?

$\boxed{}$ July

b) In 2031, the carnival will be held on 26th July.
What day of the week will 15th August 2031 be?

Monday	Tuesday	Wednesday	Thursday	Friday
☐	☐	☐	☐	☐

c) Faduma will celebrate her 17th birthday on the day of the 2031 carnival.
In what year was she born?

$\boxed{}$

(8) Look at these numbers.

0.09   1.68   0.96   0.90   0.32

a) Which of the numbers is the smallest?

0.09	1.68	0.96	0.90	0.32
☐	☐	☐	☐	☐

b) In which number does the 6 represent 6 hundredths?

0.09	1.68	0.96	0.90	0.32
☐	☐	☐	☐	☐

c) Which pair of numbers add to give 2?

$\boxed{}.\boxed{}$ and $\boxed{}.\boxed{}$

Go to the next question ⟹

9 Selasi sorts his tops into four piles.
The pictogram shows the number of tops in each pile.

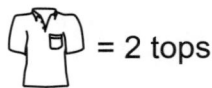

= 2 tops

Jumpers	
Formal shirts	
T-shirts	
Polo shirts	

a) How many more T-shirts than polo shirts does Selasi have?

b) Selasi gives away ¼ of his jumpers.
How many jumpers does he give away?

c) Each of Selasi's formal shirts cost the same to buy.
In total, he spent £34.50 on them. How much did each formal shirt cost?

£ ☐☐ . ☐☐

10 Fill in the answer to this calculation.

579 × 7 = ☐☐☐☐

11 Judy has bought a new fridge-freezer.
She sets the temperature in the fridge section to 4 °C
and the temperature in the freezer section to –18 °C.

a) What is the difference between the two temperatures?

☐☐ °C

b) Judy accidentally leaves the freezer door open.
The temperature in the freezer rises by 12 °C.
What is the temperature in the freezer now?

–☐☐ °C

12 Carmen has a gift card for a garden centre worth £30.
A plant that she likes costs £4.90.

a) Carmen buys 3 of these plants using the gift card.
How much money is left on the gift card?

£☐☐.☐☐

b) The price of a gnome is £15. In a sale, there is 20% off the price.
How much does the gnome cost in the sale?

£☐☐.☐☐

Go to the next question ⇨

13 Sunita has arranged some shapes into a sequence of patterns.
The first four patterns are shown below.

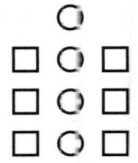

Pattern 1   **Pattern 2**   **Pattern 3**   **Pattern 4**

a) How many shapes would Sunita need to make the fifth pattern in the sequence?

13   10   15   11   9

☐   ☐   ☐   ☐   ☐

b) Sunita colours in a total of nine of the squares from Patterns 1, 2, 3 and 4.
What percentage of the squares from these four patterns has she coloured in?

☐☐ %

14 The diagram below is of Herbert's patio.

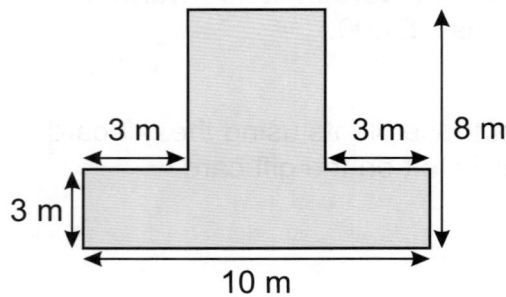

3 m   3 m   8 m

3 m

10 m

a) Work out the area of the patio.

☐☐☐ m²

b) Herbert puts a fence around the patio, leaving a 1.5 m gap for a gate.
What will be the length of the fence?

☐☐☐.☐ m

15 The grid below shows the layout of a library.

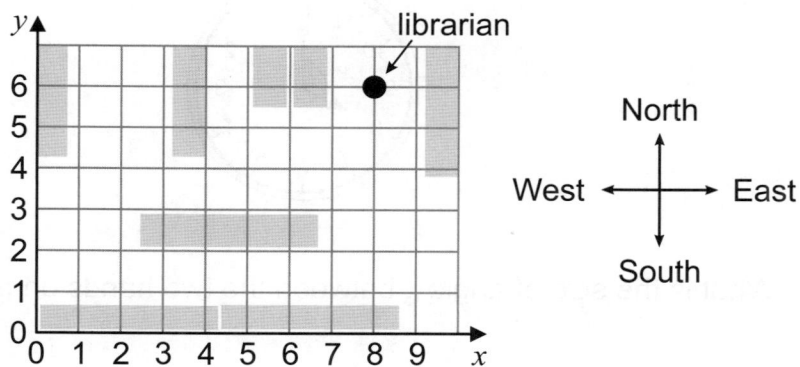

a) What are the coordinates of the librarian's position?

(☐ , ☐)

b) Beth is at the point (9, 2) and she needs a book at the point (4, 5).
Which of these describes Beth's route to the book?

▭ 3 squares south, 5 squares west

▭ 3 squares north, 5 squares east

▭ 5 squares north, 3 squares west

▭ 5 squares south, 3 squares east

▭ 3 squares north, 5 squares west

Go to the next question ⟹

(16) Look at the clock below.

a) What is the size of angle x between the two hands on the clock?

☐☐☐ °

b) Azi went to see a film one evening. The film lasted for 1 hour and 42 minutes and finished at the time shown on the clock. What time did the film start? Give your answer using the 24-hour clock.

☐☐ : ☐☐

(17) Gina is using red and gold glitter to decorate a cube. She has 8 pots of glitter.

a) She uses gold glitter on $\frac{8}{3}$ faces. How many faces is this as a mixed number?

$2\frac{2}{3}$	$1\frac{1}{3}$	$3\frac{1}{3}$	$2\frac{1}{3}$	$1\frac{2}{3}$
☐	☐	☐	☐	☐

b) Gina uses $\frac{1}{7}$ of the red glitter on one face of the cube and $\frac{3}{14}$ on another. What fraction of the red glitter does she use in total on these two faces?

$\frac{5}{7}$	$\frac{4}{14}$	$\frac{3}{7}$	$\frac{5}{14}$	$\frac{4}{21}$
☐	☐	☐	☐	☐

c) Gina uses $\frac{3}{4}$ of all the glitter she started with.
How many pots could she fill with the leftover glitter?

☐

18 Amir has drawn this Venn diagram.

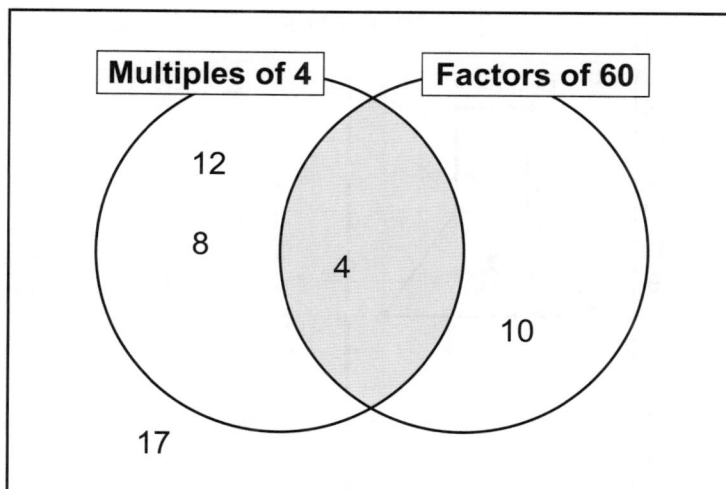

a) Which of these numbers has Amir put in the wrong place?

   4 ☐   8 ☐   10 ☐   12 ☐   17 ☐

b) Which of the following lists contains only numbers that would go in the shaded section of the diagram?

  ☐ 4, 20, 30, 60

  ☐ 4, 12, 20, 60

  ☐ 2, 12, 20, 40

  ☐ 3, 8, 12, 60

  ☐ 4, 16, 20, 60

Go to the next question ⇨

Shape X has been drawn on the grid below.

mirror line

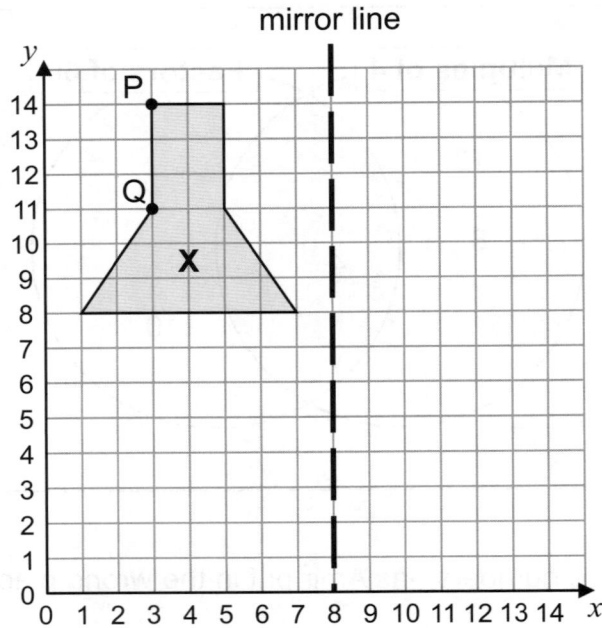

a)   What is the name of shape X?

Pentagon   Trapezium   Octagon   Hexagon   Rhombus

☐   ☐   ☐   ☐   ☐

b)   What would be the new coordinates of point P if you translated shape X five units down and seven units right?

(⬚⬚ , ⬚⬚)

c)   What would be the new coordinates of the point Q if you reflected the original shape X in the mirror line?

(⬚⬚ , ⬚⬚)

(20) The pie chart below shows the final destination of 32 trains that passed through a train station.

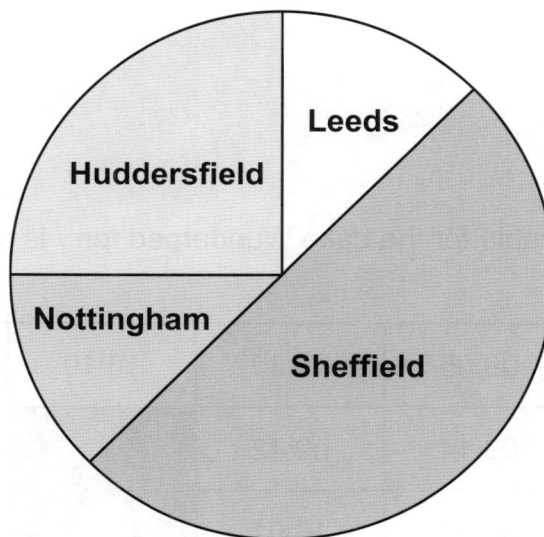

a) How many of these trains had Sheffield as their final destination?

b) What percentage of the trains had Huddersfield as their final destination?

%

(21) Barney has a stack of playing cards.

He deals out one quarter of the cards and then takes 2 cards back. He now has 20 cards in his stack.

How many cards did Barney have to start with?

Go to the next question ⟹

(22) The symbol ◇ represents a number.

If 9◇ = 81, what is the value of ◇?

◇ = ☐☐

(23) Part of the timetable for the Lake Wunderped ferry is shown below.

Lakefoot	09:05	09:30	10:10	10:30	10:55
Edelness	09:14	09:42	—	10:43	11:09
Crawlside	09:29	10:01	—	11:05	11:22
Lakecrown	09:55	10:29	10:52	11:31	—

a) Abigail boards the ferry at Edelness at 09:42 and gets off at Lakecrown.
How long is she on the ferry for?

☐☐ minutes

b) Lillian boards the 09:05 ferry from Lakefoot and gets off at Crawlside.
She spends some time in Crawlside and then boards a ferry to Lakecrown.
She arrives at Lakecrown at 11:31.

How long does she spend in Crawlside?

☐☐☐ minutes

c) Bodhi is meeting a friend in Edelness. He needs to arrive in Edelness by
half past ten. He lives 20 minutes walk away from the ferry port at Lakefoot.

What is the latest time that he can leave home to arrive in Edelness on time?

☐☐ : ☐☐

(24) The ingredients below are for a pumpkin soup recipe that will serve 8 people.

Pumpkin	2 kg
Coconut milk	560 ml
Vegetable stock	900 ml
Sunflower oil	4 teaspoons

a) How many millilitres of coconut milk would you need to make enough soup for 3 people?

[ ][ ][ ] ml

b) How many kilograms of pumpkin would you need to make enough soup for 10 people?

[ ][ ].[ ] kg

c) 1 vegetable stock cube is needed to make 400 ml of vegetable stock.
Rani is making soup for 16 people.
How many stock cubes will she need to unwrap?

[ ][ ]

Go to the next question ⇨

(25) Gilbert, Karima and Morty each own an apple orchard.
Gilbert has 36 trees in his orchard, Karima has 28 trees in her orchard
and Morty has 63 trees in his orchard.

a) Gilbert picks 61 apples from each of his trees.
How many apples has Gilbert picked in total?

b) The number of apples Karima picks from each of her trees is a square number
less than 70. She picks more apples from each tree than Gilbert.
How many apples does Karima pick from each tree?

c) The trees in Gilbert and Morty's orchards are arranged into rows of equal length.
The number of trees in each row is more than 5 and is the same in both orchards.
How many trees are in each row?

d) 15 of the trees in Gilbert's orchard were planted in the last 3 years.
What fraction of the trees in Gilbert's orchard is this?

$\frac{3}{12}$ ☐ $\frac{5}{9}$ ☐ $\frac{15}{21}$ ☐ $\frac{5}{12}$ ☐ $\frac{5}{6}$ ☐

❌ **Stop — you may check your answers in this section only**

11+ Practice Papers

For the **CEM** test

Answer Sheets

Ages 9-10

BLANK PAGE

2

© CGP 2019

Using the Multiple Choice Answer Sheets

If you're doing a Multiple Choice paper, it's often marked by a computer.
These papers use special answer sheets like the ones in this booklet.

There's a Multiple Choice answer sheet to go with each Practice Paper, so make sure you're filling in the right one. If you get used to these answer sheets now, it means there'll be no nasty surprises when you sit the real test.

Here are a few tips for using the answer sheets without getting yourself in a pickle...

Tips for Filling in the Answer Sheets

1) Before you start, fill in your name and the name of your school in the correct space. There may be boxes for other information, like your date of birth or your pupil number. Make sure you don't leave anything blank by mistake.

2) To mark your answer, put a clear pencil line through the answer box.

3) Make sure you have a pencil sharpener and an eraser for any mistakes.

4) If you make a mistake, rub out the incorrect answer first, and then fill in your new answer clearly.

5) It's easy to lose your place when you move from the practice paper to the answer sheet, so match up the question number on the paper and the answer sheet. Keeping the two sheets close together will help you do this.

6) If you skip a question to come back to later, make sure you leave a gap for that question on the answer sheet. That way your answers will stay in order.

7) Don't do rough working on your answer sheet.

8) Don't worry if you mark boxes in the same position several times in a row — just because you've marked the second box four times, it doesn't mean that your answers are wrong.

CGP

Pupil's name:

Test date:

School name:

Date of Birth

Day	Month	Year

Please mark like this: ▭

Set A: Paper 1

Pupil Number

[0] [0] [0] [0] [0] [0]
[1] [1] [1] [1] [1] [1]
[2] [2] [2] [2] [2] [2]
[3] [3] [3] [3] [3] [3]
[4] [4] [4] [4] [4] [4]
[5] [5] [5] [5] [5] [5]
[6] [6] [6] [6] [6] [6]
[7] [7] [7] [7] [7] [7]
[8] [8] [8] [8] [8] [8]
[9] [9] [9] [9] [9] [9]

School Number

[0] [0] [0] [0] [0] [0] [0]
[1] [1] [1] [1] [1] [1] [1]
[2] [2] [2] [2] [2] [2] [2]
[3] [3] [3] [3] [3] [3] [3]
[4] [4] [4] [4] [4] [4] [4]
[5] [5] [5] [5] [5] [5] [5]
[6] [6] [6] [6] [6] [6] [6]
[7] [7] [7] [7] [7] [7] [7]
[8] [8] [8] [8] [8] [8] [8]
[9] [9] [9] [9] [9] [9] [9]

Day	Month	Year
[0] [0]	January	2005
[1] [1]	February	2006
[2] [2]	March	2007
[3] [3]	April	2008
[4]	May	2009
[5]	June	2010
[6]	July	2011
[7]	August	2012
[8]	September	2013
[9]	October	2014
	November	2015
	December	2016

Section 1

EXAMPLE A
A ▭
B ▭
C ▬
D ▭

EXAMPLE B
A ▭
B ▬
C ▭
D ▭

1
A ▭
B ▭
C ▭
D ▭

2
A ▭
B ▭
C ▭
D ▭

3
A ▭
B ▭
C ▭
D ▭

4
A ▭
B ▭
C ▭
D ▭

5
A ▭
B ▭
C ▭
D ▭

6
A ▭
B ▭
C ▭
D ▭

7
A ▭
B ▭
C ▭
D ▭

8
A ▭
B ▭
C ▭
D ▭

9
A ▭
B ▭
C ▭
D ▭

10
A ▭
B ▭
C ▭
D ▭

11
A ▭
B ▭
C ▭
D ▭

12
A ▭
B ▭
C ▭
D ▭

13
A ▭
B ▭
C ▭
D ▭

14
A ▭
B ▭
C ▭
D ▭

15
A ▭
B ▭
C ▭
D ▭

Section 2

1
A ▭
B ▭
C ▭
D ▭

2
A ▭
B ▭
C ▭
D ▭

3
A ▭
B ▭
C ▭
D ▭

4
A ▭
B ▭
C ▭
D ▭

5
A ▭
B ▭
C ▭
D ▭

6
A ▭
B ▭
C ▭
D ▭

7
A ▭
B ▭
C ▭
D ▭

8
A ▭
B ▭
C ▭
D ▭

9
A ▭
B ▭
C ▭
D ▭

10
A ▭
B ▭
C ▭
D ▭

Section 3

Each word has two or more missing letters. Mark the box next to each letter that needs to be added to complete the word.

EXAMPLE

?	h	?	s	?	e	r

s ☐ l ☐ t ☐
w ■ a ☐ p ■
t ☐ i ■ m ☐

1

?	r	?	?	t	?	t	e

i ☐ a ☐ e ☐ a ☐
a ☐ r ☐ a ☐ o ☐
e ☐ l ☐ i ☐ i ☐

2

t	?	?	g	?

h ☐ u ☐ h ☐
a ☐ o ☐ s ☐
o ☐ c ☐ t ☐

3

?	e	c	?	?	m	?	n	d

f ☐ a ☐ o ☐ e ☐
r ☐ o ☐ i ☐ a ☐
k ☐ c ☐ m ☐ u ☐

4

a	?	?	?	s	t

s ☐ j ☐ i ☐
t ☐ s ☐ a ☐
b ☐ i ☐ s ☐

5

?	r	d	?	n	a	?	y

e ☐ o ☐ l ☐
u ☐ o i ☐ r ☐
o ☐ a ☐ m ☐

6

?	e	?	e	t	?	r	?

l ☐ m ☐ a ☐ i ☐
d ☐ t ☐ r ☐ y ☐
c ☐ p ☐ e ☐ s ☐

7

?	?	m	?	t

a ☐ u ☐ e ☐
s ☐ o ☐ u ☐
h ☐ d ☐ i ☐

8

a	?	?	e	?	p	?

t ☐ l ☐ m ☐ y ☐
s ☐ e ☐ l ☐ s ☐
c ☐ t ☐ g ☐ t ☐

9

s	?	?	?	e	n

c ☐ h ☐ d ☐
u ☐ d ☐ g ☐
m ☐ u ☐ e ☐

10

o	u	?	?	a	?	e	d

s ☐ e ☐ g ☐
t ☐ l ☐ m ☐
r ☐ r ☐ t ☐

11

a	?	h	?	?	v	e

s ☐ a ☐ e ☐
m ☐ i ☐ a ☐
c ☐ e ☐ i ☐

12

?	u	i	?	d

b ☐ e ☐
q ☐ l ☐
c ☐ s ☐

13

?	i	?	f	i	?	u	l	?	y

p ☐ f ☐ q ☐ s ☐
r ☐ d ☐ c ☐ l ☐
d ☐ e ☐ r ☐ t ☐

14

h	i	?	?	o	?	s

l ☐ e ☐ e ☐
d ☐ r ☐ u ☐
p ☐ i ☐ a ☐

15

v	e	?	?	?	l	e

s ☐ a ☐ l ☐
h ☐ i ☐ k ☐
m ☐ p ☐ c ☐

16

d	?	m	?	?	e

a ☐ i ☐ g ☐
i ☐ s ☐ l ☐
o ☐ a ☐ m ☐

17

d	?	c	?	?	v	e

a ☐ i ☐ v ☐
i ☐ e ☐ e ☐
e ☐ c ☐ i ☐

18

s	?	?	r	t	l	?

m ☐ u ☐ y ☐
t ☐ a ☐ s ☐
a ☐ n ☐ e ☐

19

?	a	?	t	i	?	u	s

f ☐ u ☐ s ☐
b ☐ e ☐ e ☐
c ☐ r ☐ o ☐

20

r	?	?	i	?	b	?	e

e ☐ m ☐ a ☐ e ☐
i ☐ l ☐ i ☐ a ☐
a ☐ i ☐ b ☐ l ☐

Section 4

EXAMPLE
- freckle ☐
- spot ▬
- see ☐

1
- light ☐
- luminous ☐
- bouncy ☐

2
- boot ☐
- teacher ☐
- trainer ☐

3
- become ☐
- join ☐
- chain ☐

4
- gang ☐
- fill ☐
- pack ☐

5
- shard ☐
- bit ☐
- sliced ☐

6
- win ☐
- last ☐
- latter ☐

7
- put ☐
- stand ☐
- position ☐

8
- just ☐
- equal ☐
- scarcely ☐

9
- great ☐
- brilliant ☐
- vast ☐

10
- freedom ☐
- blunt ☐
- open ☐

11
- guide ☐
- teacher ☐
- support ☐

12
- present ☐
- show ☐
- act ☐

Section 5

EXAMPLE A
- Despite ☐
- However ▬
- Also ☐
- While ☐

EXAMPLE B
- brought ☐
- drunk ☐
- travelled ☐
- arrived ▬

1
- Locates ☐
- Locate ☐
- Located ☐
- Locating ☐

2
- by ☐
- because ☐
- since ☐
- with ☐

3
- Label ☐
- Initiated ☐
- Known ☐
- Spoken ☐

4
- applaud ☐
- renowned ☐
- unknown ☐
- imagined ☐

5
- named ☐
- decided ☐
- chosen ☐
- given ☐

6
- likely ☐
- unusual ☐
- visible ☐
- possible ☐

7
- although ☐
- solely ☐
- even ☐
- never ☐

8
- found ☐
- identify ☐
- extinct ☐
- grown ☐

9
- absent ☐
- atypical ☐
- mundane ☐
- unique ☐

10
- effected ☐
- threatened ☐
- supported ☐
- dwindled ☐

11
- decided ☐
- organised ☐
- controlled ☐
- forced ☐

12
- living ☐
- home ☐
- native ☐
- discovered ☐

13
- suffered ☐
- harmed ☐
- hurt ☐
- lost ☐

14
- which ☐
- actually ☐
- thought ☐
- believing ☐

15
- bottom ☐
- surface ☐
- under ☐
- first ☐

16
- frozen ☐
- staying ☐
- wants ☐
- remains ☐

17
- frozen ☐
- warmest ☐
- melting ☐
- goes ☐

18
- heavy ☐
- thin ☐
- depth ☐
- thick ☐

Section 6

EXAMPLE A	
0.607, 0.17, 1.167, 1.76	☐
1.76, 0.607, 0.17, 1.167	☐
0.17, 0.607, 1.167, 1.76	▤
0.17, 1.76, 0.607, 1.167	☐

EXAMPLE B

    2 5 0

[0]	[0]	[0]	▬
[1]	[1]	[1]	[1]
[2]	▬	[2]	[2]
[3]	[3]	[3]	[3]
[4]	[4]	[4]	[4]
[5]	[5]	▬	[5]
[6]	[6]	[6]	[6]
[7]	[7]	[7]	[7]
[8]	[8]	[8]	[8]
[9]	[9]	[9]	[9]

1

3 tenths	☐
3 ones	☐
3 hundreds	☐
3 tens	☐
3 hundredths	☐

2 cm³

3

4.1 cm	☐
0.41 km	☐
41 cm	☐
4.1 mm	☐
41 m	☐

4

²/₅	☐
¹/₁₀	☐
¹/₅	☐
¹/₂	☐
³/₅	☐

5

6

7

8 cm²

9 %

10 .

11

⁸/₁₅	☐
⁴/₅	☐
¹¹/₁₅	☐
²/₃	☐
⁹/₁₅	☐

12

170°	☐
90°	☐
110°	☐
80°	☐
250°	☐

13 £   .

14

15 °

16 g

17

1.745	☐
1745	☐
17.45	☐
174.5	☐
17 450	☐

18 (,   )

19

1724	☐
1276	☐
1774	☐
1576	☐
1254	☐

20

$n \times n \times n$	☐
$\frac{1}{3}n$	☐
$3n$	☐
$n + 3$	☐
$3 \div n$	☐

7

© CGP 2019

Pupil's name:

Test date:

School name:

Please mark like this: ▭

Set A: Paper 2

Pupil Number	School Number		Date of Birth		

Pupil Number and School Number columns:
[0][0][0][0][0][0]
[1][1][1][1][1][1]
[2][2][2][2][2][2]
[3][3][3][3][3][3]
[4][4][4][4][4][4]
[5][5][5][5][5][5]
[6][6][6][6][6][6]
[7][7][7][7][7][7]
[8][8][8][8][8][8]
[9][9][9][9][9][9]

Date of Birth

Day	Month	Year
[0][0]	January	2005
[1][1]	February	2006
[2][2]	March	2007
[3][3]	April	2008
[4]	May	2009
[5]	June	2010
[6]	July	2011
[7]	August	2012
[8]	September	2013
[9]	October	2014
	November	2015
	December	2016

Section 1

Each word has two or more missing letters. Mark the box next to each letter that needs to be added to complete the word.

EXAMPLE A
? e ? k
p☐   u☐
w▬   i☐
l☐   a▬

1 ? ? e ? e r
c☐ n☐ p☐
i☐ l☐ v☐
b☐ f☐ m☐

2 ? a r ? ? e r
c☐ t☐ u☐
f☐ r☐ i☐
n☐ f☐ h☐

3 t ? l ? r a ? ? e
a☐ e☐ m☐ e☐
u☐ o☐ b☐ l☐
o☐ a☐ i☐ i☐

4 v a ? ? e
t☐ l☐
q☐ b☐
g☐ u☐

5 c ? n ? ? n t
o☐ b☐ e☐
a☐ t☐ i☐
e☐ s☐ u☐

6 a t ? ? ? k
m☐ e☐ a☐
i☐ s☐ c☐
t☐ a☐ i☐

7 g ? ? s ?
e☐ u☐ p☐
u☐ e☐ s☐
a☐ i☐ t☐

8 g ? n e ? a ?
i☐ s☐ r☐
e☐ p☐ m☐
a☐ r☐ l☐

9 ? i ? u i ?
l☐ d☐ d☐
s☐ q☐ l☐
f☐ m☐ e☐

10 d ? ? p ? i r
o☐ r☐ e☐
a☐ s☐ a☐
e☐ m☐ l☐

11 c ? r i ? ? s
a☐ o☐ t☐
o☐ n☐ u☐
u☐ g☐ e☐

12 l ? i ? ? r e
e☐ s☐ a☐
o☐ p☐ i☐
u☐ n☐ u☐

13 g ? ? t ? e
a☐ a☐ t☐
e☐ u☐ u☐
i☐ n☐ l☐

14 t ? ? i c a ?
y☐ e☐ t☐
o☐ p☐ l☐
r☐ m☐ d☐

15 ? o n s ? ? o u ?
t☐ c☐ i☐ t☐
c☐ h☐ s☐ r☐
r☐ i☐ e☐ s☐

16

| i | n | | ? | ? | n | s | i | | ? | ? | r | a | | ? | e |

t ☐ u ☐   m ☐ e ☐   t ☐
s ☐ o ☐   q ☐ i ☐   d ☐
c ☐ i ☐   d ☐ a ☐   s ☐

Section 2

EXAMPLE A1

2 5 0

[0] [0] [0] ■
[1] [1] [1] [1]
[2] ■ [2] [2]
[3] [3] [3] [3]
[4] [4] [4] [4]
[5] [5] ■ [5]
[6] [6] [6] [6]
[7] [7] [7] [7]
[8] [8] [8] [8]
[9] [9] [9] [9]

EXAMPLE A2

3 0

[0] ■
[1] [1]
[2] [2]
[3] ■ [3]
[4] [4]
[5] [5]
[6] [6]
[7] [7]
[8] [8]
[9] [9]

EXAMPLE A3

$\frac{1}{25}$ ☐
$\frac{1}{5}$ ■
$\frac{7}{25}$ ☐
$\frac{1}{50}$ ☐
$\frac{2}{5}$ ☐

1a

A ☐
B ☐
C ☐
D ☐
E ☐

1b

[0] [0]
[1] [1]
[2] [2]
[3] [3]
[4] [4]
[5] [5]
[6] [6]
[7] [7]
[8] [8]
[9] [9]

1c

[0] [0] [0]
[1] [1] [1]
[2] [2] [2]
[3] [3] [3]
[4] [4] [4]
[5] [5] [5]
[6] [6] [6]
[7] [7] [7]
[8] [8] [8]
[9] [9] [9]

2a

[0] [0]
[1] [1]
[2] [2]
[3] [3]
[4] [4]
[5] [5]
[6] [6]
[7] [7]
[8] [8]
[9] [9]

2b

B, D and E ☐
A, B and C ☐
C, D and E ☐
C and E ☐
B, C and D ☐

2c

C and E ☐
B and D ☐
D and E ☐
C and D ☐
B and C ☐

3a

[0] [0] [0] [0]
[1] [1] [1] [1]
[2] [2] [2] [2]
[3] [3] [3] [3]
[4] [4] [4] [4]
[5] [5] [5] [5]
[6] [6] [6] [6]
[7] [7] [7] [7]
[8] [8] [8] [8]
[9] [9] [9] [9]

3b

[0] [0] [0]
[1] [1] [1]
[2] [2] [2]
[3] [3] [3]
[4] [4] [4]
[5] [5] [5]
[6] [6] [6]
[7] [7] [7]
[8] [8] [8]
[9] [9] [9]

3c

[0] [0]
[1] [1]
[2] [2]
[3] [3]
[4] [4]
[5] [5]
[6] [6]
[7] [7]
[8] [8]
[9] [9]

3d

[0] [0] [0] [0]
[1] [1] [1] [1]
[2] [2] [2] [2]
[3] [3] [3] [3]
[4] [4] [4] [4]
[5] [5] [5] [5]
[6] [6] [6] [6]
[7] [7] [7] [7]
[8] [8] [8] [8]
[9] [9] [9] [9]

4a   mm

[0] [0] [0] [0] [0]
[1] [1] [1] [1] [1]
[2] [2] [2] [2] [2]
[3] [3] [3] [3] [3]
[4] [4] [4] [4] [4]
[5] [5] [5] [5] [5]
[6] [6] [6] [6] [6]
[7] [7] [7] [7] [7]
[8] [8] [8] [8] [8]
[9] [9] [9] [9] [9]

4b

2.8 m ☐
280 m ☐
0.28 m ☐
28 m ☐
0.028 m ☐

4c   %

[0] [0]
[1] [1]
[2] [2]
[3] [3]
[4] [4]
[5] [5]
[6] [6]
[7] [7]
[8] [8]
[9] [9]

5a

[0] [0] [0] [0]
[1] [1] [1] [1]
[2] [2] [2] [2]
[3] [3] [3] [3]
[4] [4] [4] [4]
[5] [5] [5] [5]
[6] [6] [6] [6]
[7] [7] [7] [7]
[8] [8] [8] [8]
[9] [9] [9] [9]

5b   .   m

[0] [0] [0]
[1] [1] [1]
[2] [2] [2]
[3] [3] [3]
[4] [4] [4]
[5] [5] [5]
[6] [6] [6]
[7] [7] [7]
[8] [8] [8]
[9] [9] [9]

5c

4.5 m ☐
4 m ☐
2 m ☐
3.5 m ☐
2.5 m ☐

5d

$\frac{1}{2}$ ☐
$\frac{1}{6}$ ☐
$\frac{1}{3}$ ☐
$\frac{2}{3}$ ☐
$\frac{1}{4}$ ☐

Section 2 Continued

6a
- $\frac{1}{20}$ ☐
- $\frac{2}{5}$ ☐
- $\frac{6}{25}$ ☐
- $\frac{11}{25}$ ☐
- $\frac{1}{5}$ ☐

6b %

[0]	[0]
[1]	[1]
[2]	[2]
[3]	[3]
[4]	[4]
[5]	[5]
[6]	[6]
[7]	[7]
[8]	[8]
[9]	[9]

6c .

[0]		[0]	[0]	[0]
[1]		[1]	[1]	[1]
[2]		[2]	[2]	[2]
[3]		[3]	[3]	[3]
[4]		[4]	[4]	[4]
[5]		[5]	[5]	[5]
[6]		[6]	[6]	[6]
[7]		[7]	[7]	[7]
[8]		[8]	[8]	[8]
[9]		[9]	[9]	[9]

7a
- 33 kg ☐
- 0.33 g ☐
- 3300 kg ☐
- 33 g ☐
- 3.3 kg ☐

7b . litres

[0]	[0]	[0]	[0]
[1]	[1]	[1]	[1]
[2]	[2]	[2]	[2]
[3]	[3]	[3]	[3]
[4]	[4]	[4]	[4]
[5]	[5]	[5]	[5]
[6]	[6]	[6]	[6]
[7]	[7]	[7]	[7]
[8]	[8]	[8]	[8]
[9]	[9]	[9]	[9]

7c cm

[0]	[0]
[1]	[1]
[2]	[2]
[3]	[3]
[4]	[4]
[5]	[5]
[6]	[6]
[7]	[7]
[8]	[8]
[9]	[9]

8a
- Willow ☐
- Oak ☐
- Birch ☐
- Elm ☐
- Rowan ☐
- Ash ☐

8b

[0]	[0]
[1]	[1]
[2]	[2]
[3]	[3]
[4]	[4]
[5]	[5]
[6]	[6]
[7]	[7]
[8]	[8]
[9]	[9]

8c %

[0]	[0]
[1]	[1]
[2]	[2]
[3]	[3]
[4]	[4]
[5]	[5]
[6]	[6]
[7]	[7]
[8]	[8]
[9]	[9]

8d
- £282.80 ☐
- £308 ☐
- £280.28 ☐
- £3080 ☐
- £2800 ☐

9a £ .

[0]	[0]		[0]	[0]
[1]	[1]		[1]	[1]
[2]	[2]		[2]	[2]
[3]	[3]		[3]	[3]
[4]	[4]		[4]	[4]
[5]	[5]		[5]	[5]
[6]	[6]		[6]	[6]
[7]	[7]		[7]	[7]
[8]	[8]		[8]	[8]
[9]	[9]		[9]	[9]

9b
- $5 + 5.70 \times 5 + 3.98$ ☐
- $5.70(5 + 3.98)$ ☐
- $5.70 + 3.98 \times 5$ ☐
- $5(5.70 + 3.98)$ ☐
- $5 \times 3.98 + 3.98 \times 5.70$ ☐

9c £ .

[0]	[0]		[0]	[0]
[1]	[1]		[1]	[1]
[2]	[2]		[2]	[2]
[3]	[3]		[3]	[3]
[4]	[4]		[4]	[4]
[5]	[5]		[5]	[5]
[6]	[6]		[6]	[6]
[7]	[7]		[7]	[7]
[8]	[8]		[8]	[8]
[9]	[9]		[9]	[9]

Section 3

EXAMPLE A
- a ▬
- b ☐
- c ☐
- d ☐

EXAMPLE B
- a ☐
- b ☐
- c ▬
- d ☐
- e ☐

EXAMPLE C
- a ☐
- b ▬
- c ☐
- d ☐

EXAMPLE D
- a ☐
- b ☐
- c ▬
- d ☐

EXAMPLE E
- a ☐
- b ☐
- c ▬
- d ☐

1
- a ☐
- b ☐
- c ☐
- d ☐

2
- a ☐
- b ☐
- c ☐
- d ☐

3
- a ☐
- b ☐
- c ☐
- d ☐

4
- a ☐
- b ☐
- c ☐
- d ☐

5
- a ☐
- b ☐
- c ☐
- d ☐

6
- a ☐
- b ☐
- c ☐
- d ☐

7
- a ☐
- b ☐
- c ☐
- d ☐

8
- a ☐
- b ☐
- c ☐
- d ☐
- e ☐

9
- a ☐
- b ☐
- c ☐
- d ☐
- e ☐

10
- a ☐
- b ☐
- c ☐
- d ☐
- e ☐

11
- a ☐
- b ☐
- c ☐
- d ☐
- e ☐

12
- a ☐
- b ☐
- c ☐
- d ☐
- e ☐

13
- a ☐
- b ☐
- c ☐
- d ☐
- e ☐

14
- a ☐
- b ☐
- c ☐
- d ☐
- e ☐

15
- a ☐
- b ☐
- c ☐
- d ☐

16
- a ☐
- b ☐
- c ☐
- d ☐

17
- a ☐
- b ☐
- c ☐
- d ☐

18
- a ☐
- b ☐
- c ☐
- d ☐

19
- a ☐
- b ☐
- c ☐
- d ☐

20
- a ☐
- b ☐
- c ☐
- d ☐

21
- a ☐
- b ☐
- c ☐
- d ☐

22
- a ☐
- b ☐
- c ☐
- d ☐

23
- a ☐
- b ☐
- c ☐
- d ☐

24
- a ☐
- b ☐
- c ☐
- d ☐

25
- a ☐
- b ☐
- c ☐
- d ☐

26
- a ☐
- b ☐
- c ☐
- d ☐

27
- a ☐
- b ☐
- c ☐
- d ☐

28
- a ☐
- b ☐
- c ☐
- d ☐

29
- a ☐
- b ☐
- c ☐
- d ☐

30
- a ☐
- b ☐
- c ☐
- d ☐

31
- a ☐
- b ☐
- c ☐
- d ☐

32
- a ☐
- b ☐
- c ☐
- d ☐

33
- a ☐
- b ☐
- c ☐
- d ☐

34
- a ☐
- b ☐
- c ☐
- d ☐

CGP

Pupil's name:

Test date:

School name:

Date of Birth

Day	Month	Year

Please mark like this: ▭

Set B: Paper 1

Pupil Number

[0]	[0]	[0]	[0]	[0]	[0]
[1]	[1]	[1]	[1]	[1]	[1]
[2]	[2]	[2]	[2]	[2]	[2]
[3]	[3]	[3]	[3]	[3]	[3]
[4]	[4]	[4]	[4]	[4]	[4]
[5]	[5]	[5]	[5]	[5]	[5]
[6]	[6]	[6]	[6]	[6]	[6]
[7]	[7]	[7]	[7]	[7]	[7]
[8]	[8]	[8]	[8]	[8]	[8]
[9]	[9]	[9]	[9]	[9]	[9]

School Number

[0]	[0]	[0]	[0]	[0]	[0]	[0]
[1]	[1]	[1]	[1]	[1]	[1]	[1]
[2]	[2]	[2]	[2]	[2]	[2]	[2]
[3]	[3]	[3]	[3]	[3]	[3]	[3]
[4]	[4]	[4]	[4]	[4]	[4]	[4]
[5]	[5]	[5]	[5]	[5]	[5]	[5]
[6]	[6]	[6]	[6]	[6]	[6]	[6]
[7]	[7]	[7]	[7]	[7]	[7]	[7]
[8]	[8]	[8]	[8]	[8]	[8]	[8]
[9]	[9]	[9]	[9]	[9]	[9]	[9]

Day:
[0][0]
[1][1]
[2][2]
[3][3]
[4]
[5]
[6]
[7]
[8]
[9]

Month	Year
January	2005
February	2006
March	2007
April	2008
May	2009
June	2010
July	2011
August	2012
September	2013
October	2014
November	2015
December	2016

Section 1

EXAMPLE A
A ☐
B ☐
C ▭
D ☐

EXAMPLE B
A ☐
B ▭
C ☐
D ☐

1 A B C D ☐☐☐☐
2 A B C D ☐☐☐☐
3 A B C D ☐☐☐☐
4 A B C D ☐☐☐☐
5 A B C D ☐☐☐☐

6 A B C D ☐☐☐☐
7 A B C D ☐☐☐☐
8 A B C D ☐☐☐☐
9 A B C D ☐☐☐☐
10 A B C D ☐☐☐☐
11 A B C D ☐☐☐☐
12 A B C D ☐☐☐☐
13 A B C D ☐☐☐☐
14 A B C D ☐☐☐☐

15 A B C D ☐☐☐☐
16 A B C D ☐☐☐☐
17 A B C D ☐☐☐☐
18 A B C D ☐☐☐☐
19 A B C D ☐☐☐☐
20 A B C D ☐☐☐☐

Section 2

EXAMPLE
it ☐
for ☐
time ☐
was ☐
late ▭
bed ☐

1
scissors ☐
cut ☐
when ☐
run ☐
don't ☐
holding ☐

you're ☐

2
by ☐
the ☐
is ☐
island ☐
swam ☐
only ☐

boat ☐
accessible ☐

3
piano ☐
day ☐
the ☐
many ☐
practise ☐
you ☐

every ☐
should ☐

4
tree ☐
of ☐
the ☐
jumped ☐
the ☐
squirrel ☐

climb ☐
out ☐

5
hates ☐
smelling ☐
eggs ☐
of ☐
Julie ☐
rotten ☐

taste ☐
the ☐

12

© CGP 2019

Section 2 Continued

6
health ☐	and ☐	
fruit ☐	the ☐	
enough ☐	don't ☐	
children ☐		
eat ☐		
vegetables ☐		

7
gloves ☐	got ☐	
birthday ☐	new ☐	
a ☐	I ☐	
for ☐		
hat ☐		
my ☐		

8
shining ☐	the ☐	
happy ☐	always ☐	
he ☐	is ☐	
heat ☐	sun ☐	
when ☐		
feels ☐		

9
on ☐	write ☐	
a ☐	Sunday ☐	
story ☐	short ☐	
read ☐		
night ☐		
Priya ☐		

10
could ☐	rumbling ☐	
raining ☐	the ☐	
Dima ☐	thunder ☐	
distance ☐		
hear ☐		
in ☐		

11
was ☐	really ☐	
everyone ☐	we ☐	
there ☐		
were ☐		
friendly ☐		
met ☐		

12
picture ☐	dinosaur ☐	
a ☐	of ☐	
green ☐	photograph ☐	
drew ☐		
a ☐		
Tom ☐		

13
a ☐	send ☐	
France ☐	holiday ☐	
me ☐	get ☐	
postcard ☐		
you ☐		
when ☐		

14
right ☐	the ☐	
in ☐	no ☐	
biscuits ☐	there ☐	
are ☐		
left ☐		
jar ☐		

15
roundabout ☐	the ☐	
father ☐	works ☐	
illness ☐	the ☐	
in ☐	hospital ☐	
near ☐		
my ☐		

Section 3

EXAMPLE
tiny ▬
strong ☐
large ☐
soft ☐

1
restrict ☐
grow ☐
pull ☐
advance ☐

2
rule ☐
leader ☐
follow ☐
government ☐

3
humble ☐
spiritual ☐
proper ☐
wise ☐

4
idle ☐
cosy ☐
awkward ☐
satisfactory ☐

5
cowardly ☐
ghastly ☐
stunned ☐
petrified ☐

6
present ☐
free ☐
potential ☐
used ☐

7
seeing ☐
noticeable ☐
invisible ☐
loud ☐

8
destructive ☐
threatening ☐
clumsy ☐
naughty ☐

9
expectation ☐
freedom ☐
relief ☐
opportunity ☐

10
employee ☐
qualification ☐
job ☐
specialist ☐

11
unbroken ☐
connected ☐
lengthy ☐
uncertain ☐

12
benefit ☐
blame ☐
fault ☐
calamity ☐

13
person ☐
character ☐
celebrity ☐
idol ☐

14
multiply ☐
generate ☐
prepare ☐
design ☐

15
disturb ☐
insult ☐
mourn ☐
distract ☐

16
educated ☐
logical ☐
original ☐
pessimistic ☐

17
exchange ☐
give ☐
purchase ☐
auction ☐

18
rare ☐
extravagant ☐
unbelievable ☐
mature ☐

19
break ☐
think ☐
examine ☐
notice ☐

20
consequence ☐
reason ☐
attraction ☐
aim ☐

Section 4

Each word has two or more missing letters. Mark the box next to each letter that needs to be added to complete the word.

EXAMPLE A
| p | ? | ? | n | ? | t | s |

r☐ e☐ i☐
l■ i☐ o☐
h☐ a■ e■

EXAMPLE B
| ? | h | ? | r | d |

c☐ e☐
t■ u☐
s☐ i■

EXAMPLE C
| V | ? | ? | ? | s |

i☐ r☐ a☐
e■ n■ e☐
u☐ s☐ u■

---

1 | ? | a | ? | ? | u | s |

p☐ r☐ t☐
f☐ q☐ m☐
c☐ m☐ o☐

2 | ? | l | t | ? | ? | u | ? | h |

A☐ s☐ o☐ r☐
O☐ h☐ g☐ s☐
E☐ a☐ p☐ g☐

3 | f | ? | ? | t | ? | ? | n | a | l |

a☐ r☐ s☐ u☐
i☐ c☐ t☐ o☐
u☐ n☐ i☐ n☐

4 | r | e | ? | o | ? | ? | e | d |

c☐ d☐ d☐
n☐ r☐ n☐
t☐ m☐ s☐

5 | ? | ? | i | t | ? | e | n |

r☐ i☐ t☐
s☐ r☐ s☐
w☐ a☐ b☐

6 | p | ? | i | s | ? | ? |

r☐ e☐ d☐
a☐ o☐ n☐
l☐ i☐ t☐

7 | ? | e | s | ? | r | ? | b | ? | s |

m☐ a☐ i☐ u☐
d☐ u☐ e☐ i☐
t☐ c☐ a☐ e☐

8 | h | ? | ? | r |

e☐ u☐
a☐ i☐
i☐ e☐

9 | d | ? | ? | l | a | ? | e | d |

i☐ c☐ r☐
a☐ k☐ i☐
e☐ t☐ s☐

10 | p | ? | o | ? | ? | d |

l☐ s☐ e☐
r☐ v☐ a☐
u☐ r☐ i☐

11 | A | ? | ? | o | r | ? | i | n | ? |

c☐ d☐ s☐ d☐
r☐ u☐ r☐ g☐
q☐ c☐ d☐ t☐

12 | b | ? | l | ? | ? | v | e |

u☐ a☐ e☐
e☐ i☐ a☐
i☐ e☐ i☐

13 | d | ? | ? | ? | g | ? | e | d |

e☐ u☐ i☐ h☐
a☐ s☐ g☐ s☐
i☐ n☐ e☐ n☐

14 | l | ? | ? | a | l |

i☐ y☐
a☐ s☐
o☐ t☐

15 | ? | u | ? | s | t |

s☐ i☐
q☐ r☐
p☐ e☐

16 | ? | e | ? | p | ? | t | e |

D☐ s☐ u☐
R☐ r☐ a☐
S☐ m☐ i☐

17 | f | o | ? | ? | i | d | ? | e | n |

n☐ r☐ d☐
u☐ t☐ e☐
r☐ b☐ i☐

18 | ? | ? | o | u | ? | h | t |

f☐ l☐ g☐
b☐ n☐ e☐
p☐ r☐ l☐

19 | ? | a | ? | e | d |

m☐ s☐
s☐ v☐
b☐ k☐

20 | ? | e | ? | o | ? | n | i | ? | a | b | l | e |

m☐ k☐ g☐ t☐
b☐ l☐ s☐ s☐
r☐ c☐ u☐ p☐

Section 4 Continued

21 h | ? | ? | t | o | ? | ? | c | a | l

i □ s □   u □ e □
u □ n □   r □ k □
a □ e □   o □ i □

22 ? | m | ? | g | ?

e □   a □   d □
i □   u □   e □
s □   r □   s □

Section 5

EXAMPLE A
a �
b □

EXAMPLE B
a ▬▬
b □
c □
d □

EXAMPLE C
a ▬▬
b □
c □
d □

EXAMPLE D
a □
b □
c ▬▬
d □

1
a □   d □
b □   e □
c □   f □

2
a □   d □
b □   e □
c □   f □

3
a □   d □
b □   e □
c □   f □

4
a □   d □
b □   e □
c □   f □

5
a □   d □
b □   e □
c □   f □

6
a □   d □
b □   e □
c □   f □

7
a □
b □
c □
d □

8
a □
b □
c □
d □

9
a □
b □
c □
d □

10
a □
b □
c □
d □

11
a □
b □
c □
d □

12
a □
b □
c □
d □

13
a □
b □
c □
d □

14
a □
b □
c □
d □

15
a □
b □
c □
d □

16
a □
b □
c □
d □

17
a □
b □
c □
d □

18
a □
b □
c □
d □

Set B: Paper 2

CGP

Pupil's name:

Test date:

School name:

Date of Birth

Day	Month	Year
[0] [0]	January	2005
[1] [1]	February	2006
[2] [2]	March	2007
[3] [3]	April	2008
[4]	May	2009
[5]	June	2010
[6]	July	2011
[7]	August	2012
[8]	September	2013
[9]	October	2014
	November	2015
	December	2016

Pupil Number

School Number

Please mark like this: ▭

Set B: Paper 2

Pupil Number digits: [0]–[9] (×6)
School Number digits: [0]–[9] (×6)

Section 1

EXAMPLE
- sister
- brother
- family ▬
- cousin

1
- melon
- pineapple
- mango
- carrot

2
- workbook
- notepad
- whiteboard
- diary

3
- draw
- tie
- connection
- stalemate

4
- scrubbed
- sweep
- mopped
- duster

5
- hexagon
- triangle
- pentagon
- sphere

6
- vulture
- elephant
- giraffe
- baboon

7
- astray
- route
- lost
- adrift

8
- loud
- boom
- splat
- bang

9
- wordsearch
- hangman
- hopscotch
- crossword

10
- weld
- bird
- mixture
- combine

11
- cake
- crumble
- jelly
- brownie

12
- spotless
- flawless
- invisible
- unmarked

Section 2

EXAMPLE A
- a
- b
- c
- d ▬

EXAMPLE B
- a
- b
- c
- d ▬

EXAMPLE C
- a
- b ▬
- c
- d

1 a b c d
2 a b c d
3 a b c d
4 a b c d
5 a b c d
6 a b c d
7 a b c d
8 a b c d
9 a b c d
10 a b c d
11 a b c d
12 a b c d
13 a b c d
14 a b c d
15 a b c d
16 a b c d
17 a b c d
18 a b c d

Section 3

EXAMPLE A

1	7	5	0	ml

Digits 0–9 columns with markings.

EXAMPLE B1

	2	5	0

EXAMPLE B2

3	0

EXAMPLE B3

- 1/25 ☐
- 1/5 ■
- 7/25 ☐
- 1/50 ☐
- 2/5 ☐

---

1 — two-column digit grid (0–9)

2 — five-column digit grid (0–9), unit **g**

3
- scalene ☐
- isosceles ☐
- equilateral ☐
- right-angled ☐

4
- A ☐
- B ☐
- C ☐
- D ☐
- E ☐

5
- 3/15 ☐
- 12/20 ☐
- 5/10 ☐
- 4/6 ☐
- 6/9 ☐

6
- 8919 miles ☐
- 8830 miles ☐
- 8721 miles ☐
- 8815 miles ☐
- 8829 miles ☐

7a — two-column digit grid (0–9), **July**

7b
- Monday ☐
- Tuesday ☐
- Wednesday ☐
- Thursday ☐
- Friday ☐

7c — four-column digit grid (0–9)

8a
- 0.09 ☐
- 1.68 ☐
- 0.96 ☐
- 0.90 ☐
- 0.32 ☐

8b
- 0.09 ☐
- 1.68 ☐
- 0.96 ☐
- 0.90 ☐
- 0.32 ☐

8c — digit grids: [ ] . [ ] [ ] and [ ] . [ ] [ ]

9a — two-column digit grid (0–9)

9b — two-column digit grid (0–9)

9c — £ [ ] . [ ] [ ] digit grid

10 — four-column digit grid (0–9)

11a — two-column digit grid (0–9), °C

11b — two-column digit grid (0–9), − °C

12a — £ [ ] . [ ] [ ] digit grid

12b — £ [ ] . [ ] [ ] digit grid

Section 3 Continued

13a

13 ☐
10 ☐
15 ☐
11 ☐
9 ☐

13b %

[0]	[0]
[1]	[1]
[2]	[2]
[3]	[3]
[4]	[4]
[5]	[5]
[6]	[6]
[7]	[7]
[8]	[8]
[9]	[9]

14a m²

[0]	[0]	[0]
[1]	[1]	[1]
[2]	[2]	[2]
[3]	[3]	[3]
[4]	[4]	[4]
[5]	[5]	[5]
[6]	[6]	[6]
[7]	[7]	[7]
[8]	[8]	[8]
[9]	[9]	[9]

14b . m

[0]	[0]	[0]	[ ]
[1]	[1]	[1]	[1]
[2]	[2]	[2]	[ ]
[3]	[3]	[3]	[ ]
[4]	[4]	[4]	[4]
[5]	[5]	[5]	[ ]
[6]	[6]	[6]	[6]
[7]	[7]	[7]	[7]
[8]	[8]	[8]	[ ]
[9]	[9]	[9]	[ ]

15a (,)

[0]	[0]
[1]	[1]
[2]	[2]
[3]	[3]
[4]	[4]
[5]	[5]
[6]	[6]
[7]	[7]
[8]	[8]
[9]	[9]

15b

3 squares south, 5 squares west ☐
3 squares north, 5 squares east ☐
5 squares north, 3 squares west ☐
5 squares south, 3 squares east ☐
3 squares north, 5 squares west ☐

16a °

[0]	[0]	[0]
[1]	[1]	[1]
[2]	[2]	[2]
[3]	[3]	[3]
[4]	[4]	[4]
[5]	[5]	[5]
[6]	[6]	[6]
[7]	[7]	[7]
[8]	[8]	[8]
[9]	[9]	[9]

16b :

[0]	[0]	[0]	[0]
[1]	[1]	[1]	[1]
[2]	[2]	[2]	[2]
[3]	[3]	[3]	[3]
[4]	[4]	[4]	[4]
[5]	[5]	[5]	[5]
[6]	[6]	[6]	[6]
[7]	[7]	[7]	[7]
[8]	[8]	[8]	[8]
[9]	[9]	[9]	[9]

17a

$2\frac{2}{3}$ ☐
$1\frac{1}{3}$ ☐
$3\frac{1}{3}$ ☐
$2\frac{1}{3}$ ☐
$1\frac{2}{3}$ ☐

17b

$\frac{5}{7}$ ☐
$\frac{4}{14}$ ☐
$\frac{3}{7}$ ☐
$\frac{5}{14}$ ☐
$\frac{4}{21}$ ☐

17c

[0]
[1]
[2]
[3]
[4]
[5]
[6]
[7]
[8]
[9]

18a

4 ☐
8 ☐
10 ☐
12 ☐
17 ☐

18b

4, 20, 30, 60 ☐
4, 12, 20, 60 ☐
2, 12, 20, 40 ☐
3, 8, 12, 60 ☐
4, 16, 20, 60 ☐

19a

Pentagon ☐
Trapezium ☐
Octagon ☐
Hexagon ☐
Rhombus ☐

19b (,)

[0]	[0]	[0]	[0]
[1]	[1]	[1]	[1]
[2]	[2]	[2]	[2]
[3]	[3]	[3]	[3]
[4]	[4]	[4]	[4]
[5]	[5]	[5]	[5]
[6]	[6]	[6]	[6]
[7]	[7]	[7]	[7]
[8]	[8]	[8]	[8]
[9]	[9]	[9]	[9]

19c (,)

[0]	[0]	[0]	[0]
[1]	[1]	[1]	[1]
[2]	[2]	[2]	[2]
[3]	[3]	[3]	[3]
[4]	[4]	[4]	[4]
[5]	[5]	[5]	[5]
[6]	[6]	[6]	[6]
[7]	[7]	[7]	[7]
[8]	[8]	[8]	[8]
[9]	[9]	[9]	[9]

20a

[0]	[0]
[1]	[1]
[2]	[2]
[3]	[3]
[4]	[4]
[5]	[5]
[6]	[6]
[7]	[7]
[8]	[8]
[9]	[9]

20b %

[0]	[0]
[1]	[1]
[2]	[2]
[3]	[3]
[4]	[4]
[5]	[5]
[6]	[6]
[7]	[7]
[8]	[8]
[9]	[9]

21

[0]	[0]
[1]	[1]
[2]	[2]
[3]	[3]
[4]	[4]
[5]	[5]
[6]	[6]
[7]	[7]
[8]	[8]
[9]	[9]

22

[0]	[0]
[1]	[1]
[2]	[2]
[3]	[3]
[4]	[4]
[5]	[5]
[6]	[6]
[7]	[7]
[8]	[8]
[9]	[9]

© CGP 2019

Section 3 Continued

23a ☐ ☐ minutes

[0] [0]
[1] [1]
[2] [2]
[3] [3]
[4] [4]
[5] [5]
[6] [6]
[7] [7]
[8] [8]
[9] [9]

23b ☐ ☐ ☐ minutes

[0] [0] [0]
[1] [1] [1]
[2] [2] [2]
[3] [3] [3]
[4] [4] [4]
[5] [5] [5]
[6] [6] [6]
[7] [7] [7]
[8] [8] [8]
[9] [9] [9]

23c ☐ ☐ : ☐ ☐

[0] [0]   [0] [0]
[1] [1]   [1] [1]
[2] [2]   [2] [2]
[3] [3]   [3] [3]
[4] [4]   [4] [4]
[5] [5]   [5] [5]
[6] [6]   [6] [6]
[7] [7]   [7] [7]
[8] [8]   [8] [8]
[9] [9]   [9] [9]

24a ☐ ☐ ☐ ml

[0] [0] [0]
[1] [1] [1]
[2] [2] [2]
[3] [3] [3]
[4] [4] [4]
[5] [5] [5]
[6] [6] [6]
[7] [7] [7]
[8] [8] [8]
[9] [9] [9]

24b ☐ ☐ . ☐ kg

[0] [0]   [0]
[1] [1]   [1]
[2] [2]   [2]
[3] [3]   [3]
[4] [4]   [4]
[5] [5]   [5]
[6] [6]   [6]
[7] [7]   [7]
[8] [8]   [8]
[9] [9]   [9]

24c ☐ ☐

[0] [0]
[1] [1]
[2] [2]
[3] [3]
[4] [4]
[5] [5]
[6] [6]
[7] [7]
[8] [8]
[9] [9]

25a ☐ ☐ ☐ ☐

[0] [0] [0] [0]
[1] [1] [1] [1]
[2] [2] [2] [2]
[3] [3] [3] [3]
[4] [4] [4] [4]
[5] [5] [5] [5]
[6] [6] [6] [6]
[7] [7] [7] [7]
[8] [8] [8] [8]
[9] [9] [9] [9]

25b ☐ ☐

[0] [0]
[1] [1]
[2] [2]
[3] [3]
[4] [4]
[5] [5]
[6] [6]
[7] [7]
[8] [8]
[9] [9]

25c ☐ ☐

[0] [0]
[1] [1]
[2] [2]
[3] [3]
[4] [4]
[5] [5]
[6] [6]
[7] [7]
[8] [8]
[9] [9]

25d

$3/12$ ☐
$5/9$ ☐
$15/21$ ☐
$5/12$ ☐
$5/6$ ☐

ELY5PDE1U

© CGP 2019

Using the Multiple Choice Answer Sheets

If you're doing a Multiple Choice paper, it's often marked by a computer. These papers use special answer sheets like the ones in this booklet.

There's a Multiple Choice answer sheet to go with each Practice Paper, so make sure you're filling in the right one. If you get used to these answer sheets now, it means there'll be no nasty surprises when you sit the real test.

Here are a few tips for using the answer sheets without getting yourself in a pickle...

Tips for Filling in the Answer Sheets

1) Before you start, fill in your name and the name of your school in the correct space. There may be boxes for other information, like your date of birth or your pupil number. Make sure you don't leave anything blank by mistake.

2) To mark your answer, put a clear pencil line through the answer box.

3) Make sure you have a pencil sharpener and an eraser for any mistakes.

4) If you make a mistake, rub out the incorrect answer first, and then fill in your new answer clearly.

5) It's easy to lose your place when you move from the practice paper to the answer sheet, so match up the question number on the paper and the answer sheet. Keeping the two sheets close together will help you do this.

6) If you skip a question to come back to later, make sure you leave a gap for that question on the answer sheet. That way your answers will stay in order.

7) Don't do rough working on your answer sheet.

8) Don't worry if you mark boxes in the same position several times in a row — just because you've marked the second box four times, it doesn't mean that your answers are wrong.

CGP

11+ Practice Papers

For the **CEM** test

11+

Parents' Guide

Ages 9-10

Published by CGP

Editors:

Andy Cashmore, Emma Clayton, Robbie Driscoll, Alex Fairer, Katherine Faudemer, Zoe Fenwick,
Sam Mann, Tom Miles, Alison Palin, Hannah Roscoe, Sean Walsh, Ruth Wilbourne

With thanks to Alex Fairer, Alison Griffin, Holly Robinson, Glenn Rogers and Ben Train
for the proofreading.

Please note that CGP is not associated with CEM or The University of Durham in any way. These tests
do not include any official questions and they are not endorsed by CEM or The University of Durham.
CEM, Centre for Evaluation and Monitoring, Durham University and *The University of Durham* are all
trademarks of The University of Durham.

ISBN: 978 1 78908 245 6

Printed by Elanders Ltd, Newcastle upon Tyne
Clipart from Corel®

Text, design, layout and original illustrations
© Coordination Group Publications Ltd. (CGP) 2019
All rights reserved.

Photocopying more than 5% of a paper is not permitted, even if you have a CLA licence.
Extra copies are available from CGP with next day delivery • 0800 1712 712 • www.cgpbooks.co.uk

© CGP 2019

What This Pack Contains

What this pack contains

This pack contains **four** 11+ Mixed Practice Papers for the CEM test for ages 9-10.

The questions in these papers have been written to provide age-appropriate practice, with questions written in a similar style to the real exam. They are designed to test your child's Verbal Reasoning, Comprehension, Non-Verbal Reasoning and Maths skills.

Each of the practice papers in this pack has an accompanying **multiple-choice answer sheet**, just like the answer sheets used in the real 11+ exams. There are also **full answers** to every question in the separate **answer booklet**.

You can also download and play the **online audio instructions**, which are similar to the instructions that your child will hear on test day. (Depending on the format of the test in your area, the instructions could be played as an audio recording, like the ones we have provided, or they may be read aloud by an exam invigilator.)

You can find the audio downloads at:

cgpbooks.co.uk/11plustestaudio

This set of papers also includes a **free Online Edition**. For details of how to access your Online Edition, just follow the instructions in the box below:

How to access your free Online Edition

This book includes a free Online Edition to read on your PC, Mac or tablet.
You'll just need to go to **cgpbooks.co.uk/extras** and enter this code:

2411 9648 5017 3883

By the way, this code only works for one person. If somebody else has used this book before you, they might have already claimed the Online Edition.

The pages that follow in this Parents' Guide are designed to give some guidance and information on how to best prepare for the 11+ test, as well as how to support your child in performing as well as they can.

- Before you start, it's important to remember that preparing to take the 11+ can be a stressful time for both parents and pupils. Thinking about ways in which you can minimise the pressure on your child will help to make sure that the process is as positive an experience as possible.
- By using age-appropriate practice to prepare for the 11+ test early, your child can begin to build the skills and confidence they will need to perform well when they eventually take the test.
- The practice papers in this pack allow your child to develop their Verbal Reasoning, Comprehension, Non-Verbal Reasoning and Maths 11+ skills. These skills can have a beneficial impact on your child's whole education, regardless of whether they pass the 11+ test.

© CGP 2019

What is the 11+?

It can be tricky to find reliable information about the 11+ and how to prepare for it. This page covers the basics — what the 11+ test is and how it works.

The 11+ is a selective test

Most secondary schools in the UK are comprehensive — they're non-selective and accept children of all abilities. But in some areas, selective state secondary schools (grammar schools) still exist. These schools select their pupils based on academic ability.

The 11+ test is used to determine if a child is suitable for grammar school. It's also used for entry to some independent schools. Children usually sit the test in the first term of their last year at primary school.

Some schools select pupils based just on the 11+ test results, but others look at other factors when considering an application, e.g. whether you live close to the school, or if you have other children at the school.

The format of the test varies

The exact format of the 11+ test varies depending on the school or Local Authority (LA) you're applying to, as well as on the provider that sets the test. There are two main test providers for the 11+ — **GL Assessment** and **CEM (Durham University)**. However, in some cases, the test papers will be written by the school, or by a consortium of schools in that area.

Make sure you know which of these providers is responsible for the test in your area, and find out as much information as you can about the format of the test before you start.

Wherever you are, there are four main subjects that can be tested:

> **Verbal Reasoning** — problem-solving and logic using words, letters, numbers, etc.
> **Non-Verbal Reasoning** — problem-solving and logic using pictures and symbols.
> **Maths** — often at the same level as the SATs, but it may be more challenging.
> **English** — reading comprehension, grammar and sometimes a writing task.

Tests set by GL Assessment can include any combination of these four subjects (you won't necessarily have to do all four). Traditionally, there would be a different test paper for each subject — however, some GL regions now have mixed papers, with two papers that each cover more than one subject. Check the format of the test in your region well in advance of test day.

Papers set by CEM are usually mixed, and will cover Verbal Reasoning, Non-Verbal Reasoning and Maths. However, CEM Verbal Reasoning does contain some of the same elements as GL English, such as comprehension.

The tests are usually either **multiple choice** (MC) or **standard answer** (SA) format.

> **Multiple choice** — there's a separate answer sheet. There's usually a choice of five options for each answer, and the answers may be computer-marked.
> **Standard answer** — there are spaces on the question paper for the pupil to write their own answers. There will usually not be any answer options given for the pupil to choose from.

© CGP 2019

Using the Practice Papers

This advice will help you to get the most out of this set of practice papers. You can tailor the way you use these papers to suit your child and the level they are working at.

These practice papers can be taken in multiple-choice format

There is advice on filling in the multiple-choice answer sheets on page 3 of the answer sheet booklet. Read through this advice with your child before you begin. Make sure that they understand what they need to do before they begin a paper, and that they are filling in the answer sheet which matches the paper they are attempting.

How to set the practice papers

Do the practice papers at a time when your child usually works well. This will help them work to the best of their ability. Your child should attempt the practice paper at a clear table in a quiet area, free from distractions and interruptions. They'll need a sharp pencil, an eraser and a pencil sharpener.

As the real 11+ exams may be a while off, you might want to start by helping your child to build their confidence and become familiar with the test. You could do this by:

- Taking these practice papers as an 'open-book' test. This means that, rather than sitting the papers under exam conditions, your child has access to other 11+ study materials that can help them.
- Ignoring the time limit. This will mean your child is able to concentrate on question content, without the pressure of performing under timed conditions.

Once your child feels more confident with the test style and format, you could ask them to complete a paper in test conditions.

If you do want to mimic real exam conditions, you can play the online audio content. The audio runs through the instructions found on the front of the practice paper, and will give your child information about the timings for each section. If you're not using the online audio instructions, you could read out the instructions on the front of the practice paper before your child begins, and monitor the time they are allowed for each section. Make sure that they understand what they have to do. It may help to position your child so they can see a watch or clock to help them keep track of the time they have left.

Encourage them to read over their answers if they finish within the time limit, but don't give them extra time to do this. Mark their test using the answers in the separate answer booklet.

Marking the practice papers

You should give one mark for each correct answer your child gave within the time limit, then work out the total score. There's no set pass mark for the 11+ — it will vary from school to school and year to year. However, for these practice papers, we suggest that your child aims for a score of 85% or more. If your child consistently achieves this target within the time allowed, they may be ready to try one of the practice paper packs for ages 10-11.

If they score below 85%, looking at your child's score can help you determine areas that your child struggles with. For example, if your child scored 60%, got to the end, but got 40% of the questions wrong, they need to brush up on their accuracy. If they scored 60%, got nearly all the questions right, but didn't finish the test, they need to work faster. There is further guidance on these areas on page 6.

If your child is struggling with both accuracy and timing, they could attempt the practice papers for ages 8-9 to help them build up their skills before attempting the questions targeted at 9-10.

Don't worry if your child struggles initially — the 11+ is intended to be challenging, and some of the questions will be quite different to what your child has seen before at school. The benefit of starting 11+ preparation early is that it gives plenty of time to build up their knowledge, skills and experience to be able to tackle the exams with confidence.

© CGP 2019

Improving Your Child's Score

For your child to do well in their 11+, they'll need to work quickly and avoid making mistakes. Here's some advice to help improve your child's score and test technique.

Improving accuracy

When your child is just starting out, it's a good idea to focus on their accuracy and understanding, rather than speed. You can work on their speed when they're a bit more confident.

Once your child has finished a paper and you've marked it, you should work through the questions they got wrong together, using the solutions in the answer book. That way, they will know how they should have answered those questions, and can use this knowledge when approaching similar questions in the future.

If there are particular skills or topics that your child is consistently answering incorrectly (for example, cloze questions or multiplication questions), then you can target these areas with extra practice.

Once your child has begun to improve on those weaker areas, you can keep coming back to them at regular intervals to make sure they can still get them right.

Improving speed

In the real 11+ test, children are deliberately put under time pressure. This helps schools distinguish between good candidates and the best ones. Once your child can accurately answer 11+ questions, use these tips to help them improve their speed:

- Encourage your child only to check their answers if they have time at the end of the test.
- You could introduce games to get them working faster — try using a stopwatch to time a set of questions, and encourage your child to 'beat the clock' by finishing before the time runs out.
- For comprehension questions, it's important that your child can read the text quickly. Encouraging them to read aloud at home will help provide an indicator of your child's fluency.

As your child builds up their speed, make sure they don't forget about accuracy. Working quickly can introduce the risk of making silly mistakes, such as not reading the question properly, missing a key piece of information, or recording the answer incorrectly.

Working on test technique

Your child will score better on the 11+ if they improve their test technique. Good test technique is also important for their SATs, and other exams later in their education. When they start working through assessment papers, remind them to do the following things:

- Read the front of the paper and enter the correct information on the answer sheets provided.
- Skip any questions that are really difficult, or which are taking a long time — they can come back to them if there's time at the end.
- If they can't do a question and they're running out of time, make a sensible guess. For multiple-choice questions, they may be able to rule out one or two options that definitely aren't correct, which gives a better chance of guessing which of the remaining options is right.

If your child's test is in multiple-choice format, there are some other specific techniques to practise:

- Marking the correct box neatly and quickly using a horizontal line.
- Making sure they mark the answer in the correct box, especially if they skip a question.
- If they don't finish the paper, filling in the rest of the answers randomly.

It's a good idea to practise good exam technique and get your child used to working in test conditions. That way, your child will be well prepared when the time comes to sit the real exam.

© CGP 2019

How to Approach the Test

As well as making sure your child can answer 11+ questions quickly and accurately, you should also focus on your approach to the test itself. By encouraging your child to see the 11+ positively, you can help them to approach the test in a way that will maximise their chances of scoring highly.

Staying positive

If you're starting to prepare your child for the 11+ early, the test can seem a long way off. Preparation for the test can be stressful, so it's important to try to make your child's experience a positive one.

When doing practice papers, any low scores should be approached with a positive attitude. You could encourage your child to view them as an opportunity to pinpoint any strengths and weaknesses, otherwise it'll be easy for them to focus on the negatives. Areas for improvement can then be targeted in order to do better next time.

Rewarding your child for their hard work can help to keep them motivated. Positively reinforcing the effort they are putting in will encourage them to persevere with their test preparation.

Planning your approach

Ideally, your child should be working at 11+ standard well before they sit the test. Consider when they might be ready to attempt some questions levelled for 10-11 standard — it may be useful to create a timeline so that you can plan how your child can build their skills throughout their preparation.

You could use a star chart to reward your child's progress. This could help them to keep track of how well they are doing, as well as helping to keep them motivated.

If your child struggles with the practice materials in this pack, they may need to use materials targeted at a lower age range. The age ranges stated on practice materials give some guidance on their difficulty level. Older children can still benefit from using 8-9 resources if they need to develop their skills. Equally, if your child finds the materials targeted at their age range too easy, they may be ready to try materials aimed at a slightly higher level.

Fun ways to improve

It's important that 11+ practice doesn't start to feel like a chore, especially if your child is beginning to prepare for the test early. There are lots of activities and games that you can use to help your child continue to develop skills they will need for the 11+. These might include:

- Completing puzzles such as tangrams. This will help them to develop their spatial awareness.
- Reading a variety of fiction and non-fiction texts. This will help your child become familiar with different writing styles and build up a wide vocabulary.
- Playing word games or crosswords in puzzle books or on the internet.
- Writing stories, letters to friends or newspaper articles inspired by interesting headlines.
- Practising number puzzles such as Kakuro. This will help to develop your child's maths skills.

The right school for your child

If your child is really struggling with 11+ preparation, it might be worth considering whether or not your child is suited to grammar school. Sitting the 11+ is a choice and you can withdraw your child from the process at any point if you decide grammar school might not be for them.

Speak to your child and find out their opinions. They may have concerns about grammar school that you can talk to them about. A grammar school environment does not suit every learner — remember that there are many excellent comprehensive schools where your child can be happy and successful.

© CGP 2019

CGP

11+ Practice Paper

For Ages 9-10

Set A: Paper 1

For the CEM Test

© CGP 2019

Read the following:

Do not open this booklet or start the test until you are told to do so.

1. This test can be taken in either multiple-choice or write-in format.

2. If you are taking it as a multiple-choice test, you should mark your answer to each question in pencil on the separate answer sheet. Mark the correct box quickly and neatly using a horizontal line.

3. If you are taking it as a write-in test, you should write your answer to each question in pencil on the paper. Write your answer carefully in the space provided or, if there is a range of options, mark the correct box quickly and neatly using a horizontal line.

4. If you make a mistake, rub it out and mark your new answer clearly.

5. There are six sections in this test.

6. The time allowed for each section is given at the start of that section. You will have a total of 45 minutes to complete the timed sections of the test.

7. Each section includes examples showing you how to answer the questions. You may refer to these examples at any time as you work through the section.

8. Do as many questions as you can. For some questions you will be given a range of options — if you get stuck on one of these questions, choose the answer that you think is most likely to be correct, then move on to the next question. If you get stuck on a question for which no options are given, leave it and move on to the next question. If you have time at the end of the section, go back and have another go at the questions you could not answer.

9. You should do any rough working on a separate piece of paper.

Work carefully, but go as quickly as you can.

© CGP 2019

Example Read these example questions. You may return to these examples at any time as you work through this section.

HMS Iolaire — A Tragedy Follows a Victory

1   World War I had just ended, the Armistice had been agreed, and a large number of sailors were making their way home to Stornoway on the island of Lewis, off the west coast of Scotland. They were looking forward to coming home.

     However, in the early hours of January 1st, 1919, disaster struck. HMS Iolaire crashed
5   into the notorious 'Beasts of Holm', a set of rocks just a mile away from the safety of Stornoway harbour. Around 50 men jumped overboard, planning to swim the short distance to the shore. Sadly, the stormy seas and windy conditions meant that these men perished. Meanwhile, there were many fatalities on board as the ship began to sink. The alarm was raised and the town's coastguard was called out, but by the time he and his team arrived at
10   the scene of the disaster, the ship had sunk.

(A)   Why did the sailors have to travel to Stornoway by boat?

⬜ **A**   Because Stornoway is on the west coast of Scotland
⬜ **B**   Because they were on their way back from World War I
▰ **C**   Because Stornoway is on an island
⬜ **D**   Because the 'Beasts of Holm' were dangerous

(B)   The 'Beasts of Holm' are described as "notorious" (line 5). What is meant by this?

⬜ **A**   The rocks were concealed from view.
▰ **B**   The rocks were well known for being dangerous.
⬜ **C**   Many people admired the rocks.
⬜ **D**   The rocks had a mysterious reputation.

End of example questions

⚠ **Wait until you are told to go on** ⚠

There are 15 questions in this section

Read the passage carefully and then answer the questions that follow.

An adapted extract from 'The Carved Lions'

1   I was a very straightforward child. I thought it would be *nice* to have more money, so that mamma would not need to be so busy and could have more pretty dresses, and above all that we could then live in the country, but I never minded being poor in any sore or ashamed way. And I often envied my brother, Haddie, who did go to school. I thought

5   it would be nice to have lots of other little girls to play with. I remember once saying so to mamma, but she shook her head.

    "I don't think you would like it as much as you think you would," she said. "Not at present at least. When you are a few years older I hope to send you to some classes at Miss Ledbury's school, and by that time you will enjoy her good teaching. But I am quite

10   sure it is better and happier for you to be at home, even though you find it rather lonely sometimes."

    Our house was a short distance from the centre of the town, where the best shops were. We were very fond of going to the shops with mamma. We thought them very grand and beautiful, though they were not nearly as pretty as shops are nowadays, for they were

15 much smaller and darker, so that the things could not be spread out in the attractive way they are now, nor were the things themselves nearly as varied and tempting.

    There was one shop which interested us very much. It belonged to the principal furniture-maker of Mexington. It scarcely looked like a shop, but was more like a rather gloomy private house very full of heavy dark cabinets and tables and wardrobes and

20 chairs, mostly of mahogany, and all extremely good and well made. Yes, furniture, though ugly, really was very good in those days — I have one or two relics of my old home still, in the shape of a leather-covered arm-chair and a beautifully-made chest of drawers. For mamma's godmother had helped to furnish our house when we came to Mexington, and she was the sort of old lady who when she gave you a present gave you the very best.

25 She had had furniture herself made by Cranston — that was the cabinet-maker's name — and it had been first-rate, so she ordered what she gave mamma from him also.

    But it was not because the furniture was so good that we liked going to Cranston's. It was for quite another reason. A little way in from the front entrance to the shop, where there were glass doors to swing open, stood a pair of huge lions carved in very dark,

30 almost black, wood. They were nearly, if not quite, as large as life, and the first time I saw them, when I was only four or five, I was really frightened of them. They guarded the entrance to the inner part of the shop, which was dark and gloomy and mysterious-looking,

Passage continues over the page ⇨

and I remember clutching hold of mamma's hand as we passed them, not feeling at all sure

that they would not suddenly spring forward and catch us. But when mamma saw that I was

35 frightened, she stopped and made me feel the lions and stroke them to show me that they

were only wooden and could not possibly hurt me. And after that I grew very fond of them,

and was always asking her to take me to the "lion shop."

Haddie liked them too — his great wish was to climb on one of their backs and pretend

to be going for a ride. I don't think I thought of that. What I liked was to stroke their heavy

40 manes and think to myself what I would do if, all of a sudden, one of them "came alive".

So, for one reason or another, both Haddie and I were always very pleased when mamma

had to make a visit to Cranston's.

This happened oftener than might have been expected, considering that our house

was small, and that my father and mother were not rich enough often to buy new furniture.

45 For mamma's godmother seemed to be always ordering something or other at the

cabinet-maker's, and as she knew mamma was very sensible and careful, she used to write

to her to explain to Cranston about the things she wanted, or to look at them before he sent

them home, to see that they were all right. And Cranston was always very polite indeed to

mamma.

50 He himself was a stout, red-faced, little, elderly man, with gray whiskers, which he

brushed up in a fierce kind of way that made him look like a rather angry cat, though he

really was a very gentle and kind old man. I thought him much nicer than his partner, whose

name was Berridge, a tall, thin man, who talked very fast, and made a great show of scolding

any of the clerks or workmen who happened to be about.

55 Mr. Cranston was very proud of the lions. They had belonged to his grandfather and then

to his father, who had both been in the same sort of business as he was, and he told mamma

they had been carved in "the East." I didn't know what he meant by the East, and I don't now

know what country he was alluding to — India or China or Japan. And I am not sure that he

knew himself. No doubt, wherever they came from, the lions were very beautifully carved.

by Mary Louisa Molesworth

_____

Answer these questions about the text. You can refer back to the text if you need to.
Pick the best answer and draw a line through the rectangle next to it.

1 Which of the following statements about the narrator is true?

- ☐ **A** She wanted to be rich when she was younger.
- ☐ **B** She was embarrassed by how little money her family had.
- ☐ **C** She wasn't bitter about her family's poverty.
- ☐ **D** She thought that it was better to be poor than rich.

2 According to the text, what is the main reason why the narrator wanted to go to school?

- ☐ **A** She wanted to be with her brother.
- ☐ **B** She wanted to learn new things.
- ☐ **C** She wanted to make new friends.
- ☐ **D** She wanted to get out of the house more.

3 What reason does the narrator's mother give for her not going to school?

- ☐ **A** She thought that she wouldn't enjoy it.
- ☐ **B** She couldn't afford to send her to school.
- ☐ **C** She thought that she would prefer being on her own.
- ☐ **D** She didn't think that there was a good school nearby.

4 What does the narrator think about the quality of the shops during her childhood?

- ☐ **A** The shops were grander when she was a child.
- ☐ **B** The shops were not as visually appealing as they are now.
- ☐ **C** The shops offered a greater range of goods when she was young.
- ☐ **D** There were fewer shops during her childhood.

5 What does it mean when the narrator says "I have one or two relics of my old home" (line 21)?

- ☐ **A** She remembers some of the furniture that her family used to have.
- ☐ **B** She still has some pictures of her old house.
- ☐ **C** She has bought new furniture that looks like her old furniture.
- ☐ **D** She has kept some of the furniture from when she was a child.

Go to the next question ⇨

6   Why do you think the narrator and her brother liked visiting Cranston's shop?

       ☐ **A**   The shop was grand and beautiful.
       ☐ **B**   Mr. Cranston was a better cabinet-maker than his competitors.
       ☐ **C**   It didn't look like a shop at all.
       ☐ **D**   There were two particular items that they liked going to see.

7   Which of the following best describes the narrator's initial reaction to the carved lions?

       ☐ **A**   She was overjoyed.
       ☐ **B**   She was uneasy.
       ☐ **C**   She was fascinated.
       ☐ **D**   She was confused.

8   Why did the narrator's mother visit Mr. Cranston's shop quite often?

       ☐ **A**   She was friends with Mr Cranston.
       ☐ **B**   She liked looking at the furniture.
       ☐ **C**   She went on behalf of her godmother.
       ☐ **D**   She knew that her children liked looking at the lions.

9   Which of the following is not mentioned in the text?

       ☐ **A**   The weight of the carved lions
       ☐ **B**   The colour of the carved lions
       ☐ **C**   The material the lions were carved out of
       ☐ **D**   The number of carved lions

10   The narrator says that Berridge "made a great show of scolding" his workers (line 53).
       This suggests that:

       ☐ **A**   he didn't really scold them at all.
       ☐ **B**   he wanted people to see what he was doing.
       ☐ **C**   he was a good manager.
       ☐ **D**   his workers listened to him.

(11) Which of the following statements is false?

- [ ] **A** The narrator liked Mr Cranston more than Mr Berridge.
- [ ] **B** Mr. Cranston paid a lot of money for the lions.
- [ ] **C** Mr. Cranston's grandfather worked in the furniture business.
- [ ] **D** The narrator wasn't sure where the lions came from.

(12) What does "principal" (line 17) mean?

- [ ] **A** Only
- [ ] **B** Oldest
- [ ] **C** Main
- [ ] **D** Cheapest

(13) Mr. Cranston's furniture is described as "first-rate" (line 26). This means that:

- [ ] **A** the furniture arrived quickly.
- [ ] **B** the furniture was very expensive.
- [ ] **C** the furniture was good quality.
- [ ] **D** the furniture looked nice.

(14) What does "stout" (line 50) mean?

- [ ] **A** Short
- [ ] **B** Overweight
- [ ] **C** Clever
- [ ] **D** Humble

(15) What does "alluding to" (line 58) mean?

- [ ] **A** Guessing at
- [ ] **B** Referring to
- [ ] **C** Travelling to
- [ ] **D** Lying about

Ⓧ Stop — you may check your answers in this section only

There are 10 questions in this section

Read the passage carefully and then answer the questions that follow.

The London Underground

1   The London Underground is not only the oldest underground rail network in the world, it's
also one of the largest and busiest. However, the city's underground rail network was not always
as enormous as it is now. On 10th January 1863, London's first underground passenger railroad
(known as the Metropolitan Railway) was opened between Paddington and Farringdon. It only
5   spanned around four miles, but it was the first of its kind in the world.

The opening of the Metropolitan Railway was just one of several landmark moments in the
history of underground rail travel. In 1869, trains crossed under the River Thames for the first
time via the Thames Tunnel. Designed and built by the engineer Marc Brunel and his son
Isambard, the tunnel was less than half a mile long and was initially used as a foot tunnel. It
10   attracted many visitors from its opening in 1843 until it was bought by the East London Railway
Company in 1865. London continued to be the only city to operate underground passenger
trains until 1896, when the Budapest Metro and the Glasgow Subway were both opened. The
Budapest Metro even used electricity to power its trains — a method that had first been used to
power underground trains in London six years earlier.

15   Over time, the various underground railroads in London became a single rail network known
as the London Underground. At the start of the 20th century, the London Underground began to
develop its own brand. Today, the famous circular logo can be found on a range of merchandise
which is sold around the world. These sales help to provide extra income for London's transport
services. Nearly a quarter of a century after the logo was designed, an early version of the now
20   iconic Tube map was created. The map is designed to look like an electrical circuit, and it is
estimated that even today, around 30% of passengers take longer journeys than they need to
because it is not to scale.

However, there was once a time when thousands of Londoners arrived at Underground
stations without intending to travel anywhere at all. During World War II, some stations were
25   used as air-raid shelters and supply trains were set up to bring hot drinks to the roughly 175 000
Londoners who slept beneath the streets of London. Meanwhile, other stations were used to
protect artefacts which came from the British Museum, or for various military purposes.

Today, London still boasts one of the biggest underground rail networks in the world by length,
with its 402 km of track being dwarfed only by China's Shanghai and Beijing metros in 2018. With
30   the city's population still increasing, it's likely that the Underground will only continue to grow.

Answer these questions about the text. You can refer back to the text if you need to.
Pick the best answer and draw a line through the rectangle next to it.

(1) According to the text, which of these statements cannot be true?

- ☐ **A** The London Underground is the world's oldest underground rail network.
- ☐ **B** Paddington and Farringdon are both in London.
- ☐ **C** The world's first underground train journey was underneath the Thames.
- ☐ **D** London's underground rail network has grown substantially.

(2) How long was the Thames Tunnel open for before it was bought by the East London Railway Company?

- ☐ **A** 6 years
- ☐ **B** 11 years
- ☐ **C** 22 years
- ☐ **D** 30 years

(3) According to the text, which of these statements is true?

- ☐ **A** The Metropolitan Railway was built by Marc and Isambard Brunel.
- ☐ **B** The Metropolitan Railway was longer than the Thames Tunnel.
- ☐ **C** The opening of the Metropolitan Railway wasn't that important.
- ☐ **D** The opening of the Metropolitan Railway took place in the late 1860s.

(4) What kind of traffic would have been travelling through the Thames Tunnel in 1860?

- ☐ **A** Pedestrians only
- ☐ **B** Trains only
- ☐ **C** Pedestrians and trains
- ☐ **D** Neither pedestrians nor trains

(5) When did London first start operating electric underground passenger trains?

- ☐ **A** 1865
- ☐ **B** 1890
- ☐ **C** 1896
- ☐ **D** 1902

Go to the next question ⇨

6 In how many different cities was it possible to take underground rail travel at the end of the 19th century?

- ☐ **A**   None
- ☐ **B**   One
- ☐ **C**   Two
- ☐ **D**   Three or more

7 According to the text, why do around 30% of passengers take longer journeys than needed?

- ☐ **A**   The passengers don't understand electrical circuits.
- ☐ **B**   The Tube map doesn't provide an accurate representation of distances.
- ☐ **C**   The Tube map isn't large enough for people to understand.
- ☐ **D**   The designer wanted the Tube map to be a challenge for passengers.

8 According to the text, one of the ways the London Underground is able to generate money on top of ticket sales is by:

- ☐ **A**   leasing stations to the army.
- ☐ **B**   gathering donations from passengers.
- ☐ **C**   selling branded products.
- ☐ **D**   protecting artefacts belonging to the British Museum.

9 Why did people sleep in Underground stations during the war?

- ☐ **A**   They were working in military offices based there.
- ☐ **B**   They wanted to catch early trains.
- ☐ **C**   They were hiding from bombs.
- ☐ **D**   They were trapped there by falling rubble.

10 According to the text, where must the second longest rail network in the world be located?

- ☐ **A**   China
- ☐ **B**   Beijing
- ☐ **C**   Shanghai
- ☐ **D**   London

ⓧ Stop — you may check your answers in this section only

BLANK PAGE

© CGP 2019

Section 3: Verbal Reasoning — Synonyms

Example Read this example question. You may return to this example at any time as you work through this section.

Complete the word on the right so that it means the same, or nearly the same, as the word on the left.

A mumble   w h i s p e r

⚠️ **Wait until you are told to go on** ⚠️

⏱ **You have 6 minutes to complete this section** ⏱

There are 20 questions in this section

Complete the word on the right so that it means the same, or nearly the same, as the word on the left.

1 annoy   ☐ r ☐ t ☐ t e

2 hard   t ☐ ☐ g ☐

3 advise   ☐ e c ☐ m ☐ n d

4 help   a ☐ ☐ ☐ s t

5 normal   ☐ r d ☐ n a ☐ y

6 graveyard ☐ e ☐ e t ☐ r ☐

7 confess   ☐ ☐ m ☐ t

8 try   a ☐ ☐ e ☐ p ☐

9 unexpected   s ☐ ☐ ☐ e n

10 angry   o u ☐ ☐ a ☐ e d

11 accomplish   a ☐ h ☐ ☐ v e

12 make   ☐ u ☐ i ☐ d

13 trouble   ☐ i ☐ f i ☐ u l ☐ y

14 ugly   h i ☐ ☐ o ☐ s

15 car   v e ☐ ☐ ☐ l e

16 break   d ☐ m ☐ ☐ e

17 trick   d ☐ c ☐ ☐ v e

18 shock   s ☐ ☐ r t l ☐

19 careful   ☐ a ☐ t i ☐ u s

20 trustworthy   r ☐ ☐ i ☐ b ☐ e

❌ **Stop — you may check your answers in this section only**

Example Read this example question. You may return to this example at any time as you work through this section.

Choose the word which has a similar meaning to the words in both sets of brackets.

A (find   discover)   (stain   blemish)   freckle   spot   see
                                                      ☐   ▬   ☐

⚠️ **Wait until you are told to go on** ⚠️

🕐 **You have 4 minutes to complete this section** 🕐

There are 12 questions in this section

Choose the word which has a similar meaning to the words in both sets of brackets.

1 (sunny   glowing)   (lantern   beacon)   light   luminous   bouncy
                                                      ☐   ☐   ☐

2 (sneaker   shoe)   (instructor   coach)   boot   teacher   trainer
                                                      ☐   ☐   ☐

3 (enlist   enroll)   (link   connect)   become   join   chain
                                                       ☐   ☐   ☐

4 (cram   load)   (bunch   collection)   gang   fill   pack
                                                      ☐   ☐   ☐

5 (chewed   gnawed)   (piece   part)   shard   bit   sliced
                                                       ☐   ☐   ☐

6 (final concluding)   (survive prevail)   win last latter
☐   ☐   ☐

7 (posture stance)   (place spot)   put stand position
☐   ☐   ☐

8 (fair impartial)   (hardly barely)   just equal scarcely
☐   ☐   ☐

9 (terrific excellent)   (enormous large)   great brilliant vast
☐   ☐   ☐

10 (honest frank)   (unlock release)   freedom blunt open
☐   ☐   ☐

11 (mentor tutor)   (direct lead)   guide teacher support
☐   ☐   ☐

12 (display demonstrate)   (spectacle performance)   present show act
☐   ☐   ☐

⊗ Stop — you may check your answers in this section only

Section 5: Verbal Reasoning — Cloze

Example Read these example questions. You may return to these examples at any time as you work through this section.

Tea is often thought of as a traditional English drink. **A** ☐ Despite / ☑ However / ☐ Also / ☐ While , it was popular in

China centuries before it **B** ☐ brought / ☐ drunk / ☐ travelled / ☑ arrived in Europe.

⚠ **Wait until you are told to go on** ⚠

🕕 **You have 6 minutes to complete this section** 🕕

There are 18 questions in this section

1 ☐ Locates / ☐ Locate / ☐ Located / ☐ Locating in Siberia, a region found in the east of Russia, Lake Baikal is

the largest freshwater lake in the world **2** ☐ by / ☐ because / ☐ since / ☐ with volume. **3** ☐ Label / ☐ Initiated / ☐ Known / ☐ Spoken as

the 'Pearl of Siberia', the lake is **4** ☐ applaud / ☐ renowned / ☐ unknown / ☐ imagined for its breathtaking views and was

5 ☐ named / ☐ decided / ☐ chosen / ☐ given a UNESCO World Heritage Site in 1996. Lake Baikal boasts famously

clear waters and it is sometimes **6** ☐ likely / ☐ unusual / ☐ visible / ☐ possible to see the bottom of the lake,

(7)
- [ ] although
- [ ] solely
- [ ] even
- [ ] never

at great depths. Over 2000 species of plants and animals can be

(8)
- [ ] found
- [ ] identify
- [ ] extinct
- [ ] grown

in the lake, most of which are

(9)
- [ ] absent
- [ ] atypical
- [ ] mundane
- [ ] unique

to the area. However,

in recent years, this wildlife has become

(10)
- [ ] effected
- [ ] threatened
- [ ] supported
- [ ] dwindled

by human factors, such as

fishing and pollution. In 2017, the government was

(11)
- [ ] decided
- [ ] organised
- [ ] controlled
- [ ] forced

to ban the fishing

of omul (a type of fish

(12)
- [ ] living
- [ ] home
- [ ] native
- [ ] discovered

only to Baikal) for profit. Much of the wildlife

has

(13)
- [ ] suffered
- [ ] harmed
- [ ] hurt
- [ ] lost

from algal blooms,

(14)
- [ ] which
- [ ] actually
- [ ] thought
- [ ] believing

to be caused by pollution

from nearby towns. In January, the

(15)
- [ ] bottom
- [ ] surface
- [ ] under
- [ ] first

of Lake Baikal freezes over. The ice

(16)
- [ ] frozen
- [ ] staying
- [ ] wants
- [ ] remains

on the lake for around five months, before

(17)
- [ ] frozen
- [ ] warmest
- [ ] melting
- [ ] goes

again

around May or June. The ice on the lake can be over a metre

(18)
- [ ] heavy
- [ ] thin
- [ ] depth
- [ ] thick

, and is so

strong that for part of the year, the lake can even be used as a road.

⊗ Stop — you may check your answers in this section only

Example Read these example questions. You may return to these examples at any time as you work through this section.

A Arrange these numbers in order from smallest to largest:

1.167   0.17   0.607   1.76

☐   0.607,   0.17,   1.167,   1.76
☐   1.76,   0.607,   0.17,   1.167
▰   0.17,   0.607,   1.167,   1.76
☐   0.17,   1.76,   0.607,   1.167

B Dustin counted the number of guests staying at his hotel over five months. He made a bar chart of his results.

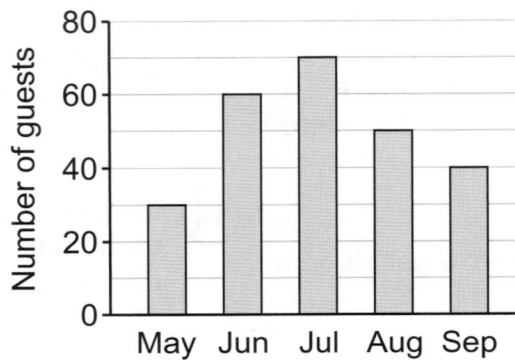

How many guests were there in total over the five months?

2 5 0

End of example questions

There are 20 questions in this section

1 Which of the following is the value of the 3 in 132.64?

3 tenths ☐   3 ones ☐   3 hundreds ☐   3 tens ☐   3 hundredths ☐

2 Ekisha makes this 3D shape from 1 cm³ blocks.

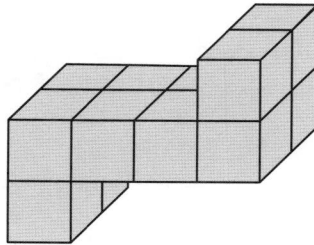

What is the volume of Ekisha's shape?

☐☐ cm³

3 Which of these is the best estimate for the height of a hen?

4.1 cm ☐   0.41 km ☐   41 cm ☐   4.1 mm ☐   41 m ☐

4 A diagram of a honeycomb is shown below.
The area of the honeycomb that is filled with honey is shaded.

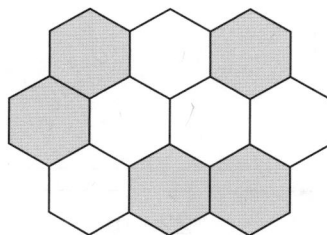

What fraction of the honeycomb is filled?

²⁄₅ ☐   ¹⁄₁₀ ☐   ¹⁄₅ ☐   ¹⁄₂ ☐   ³⁄₅ ☐

Go to the next question ⇨

5 $7 \times ? = 420$

What number should replace the ? to make this calculation correct?

6 Mike, Lucas and Nadya have 150 football stickers between them.
Mike has 72 stickers and Lucas has 46 stickers.
How many stickers does Nadya have?

7 The first five terms in a sequence are:

1    $\boxed{?}$ 13   19   25

What number goes in the box to complete the sequence?

8 Keiko makes a birthday card for her friend by
folding the shape below in half along the middle.

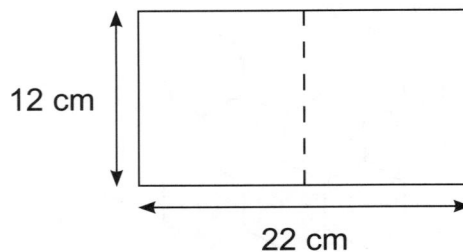

12 cm

22 cm

What will the area of the front of the birthday card be?

cm²

20

© CGP 2019

9 Helena cuts these shapes from a piece of paper.

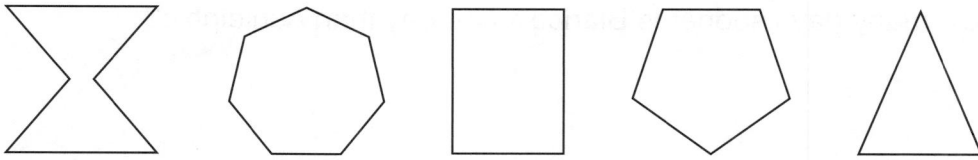

What percentage of the shapes are irregular polygons?

☐☐ %

10 Round 5.94 to the nearest tenth.

☐.☐

11 Which of these fractions is the largest?

$\frac{8}{15}$ $\frac{4}{5}$ $\frac{11}{15}$ $\frac{2}{3}$ $\frac{9}{15}$

☐   ☐   ☐   ☐   ☐

12 Look at the angle below.

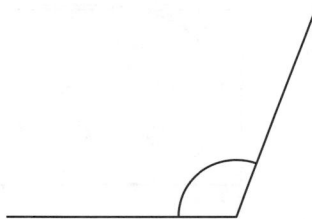

Which of the following is the size of this angle?

170°   90°   110°   80°   250°

☐   ☐   ☐   ☐   ☐

13 A souvenir shop sells keyrings for £1.40 and pens for £2.75.
Haseem buys three keyrings and one pen.
How much does he spend in total?

£ ☐☐.☐☐

Go to the next question ➡

(14) Ashleigh's birthday is 5^3 days from now.
Bianca's birthday is 4^3 days from now.
How many days sooner is Bianca's birthday than Ashleigh's?

☐☐☐

(15) Look at the angles below.

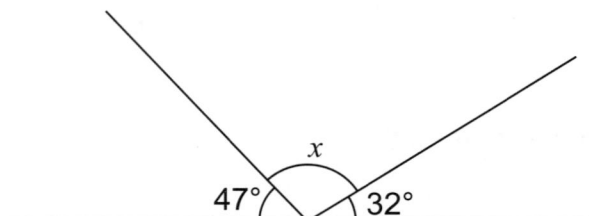

What is the size of the missing angle x?

☐☐☐°

(16) Irena has the amount of flour shown on the scales.

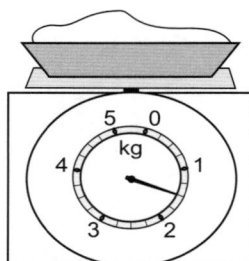

She uses 680 g of the flour to make a loaf of bread.
How many grams of flour does Irena have left?

☐☐☐☐ g

(17) $349 \times 50 = 17\,450$

What is 3.49×5?

1.745	1745	17.45	174.5	17450
☐	☐	☐	☐	☐

18 Three corners of a rectangle are marked on the grid below.

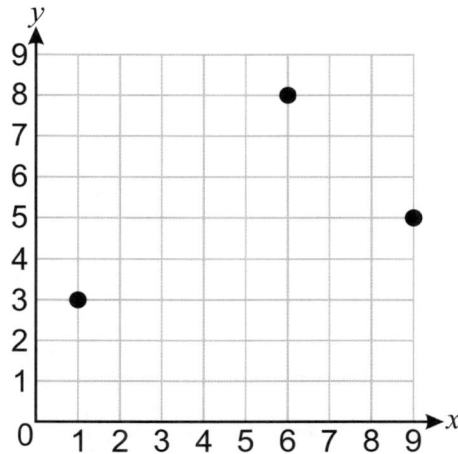

What are the coordinates of the rectangle's missing corner?

(☐ , ☐)

19 Josh has traced his family history back to the year MDCCLXXIV.
What is this year represented in figures?

1724	1276	1774	1576	1254
☐	☐	☐	☐	☐

20 Nico caught n fish on a fishing trip.
Tyler caught three more fish than Nico.
Which expression gives the number of fish Tyler caught?

$n \times n \times n$	$\frac{1}{3}n$	$3n$	$n + 3$	$3 \div n$
☐	☐	☐	☐	☐

BLANK PAGE

24

© CGP 2019

11+ Practice Paper

For Ages 9-10

Set B: Paper 1

For the CEM Test

Read the following:

Do not open this booklet or start the test until you are told to do so.

1. This test can be taken in either multiple-choice or write-in format.

2. If you are taking it as a multiple-choice test, you should mark your answer to each question in pencil on the separate answer sheet. Mark the correct box quickly and neatly using a horizontal line.

3. If you are taking it as a write-in test, you should write your answer to each question in pencil on the paper. Write your answer carefully in the space provided or, if there is a range of options, mark the correct box quickly and neatly using a horizontal line.

4. If you make a mistake, rub it out and mark your new answer clearly.

5. There are five sections in this test.

6. The time allowed for each section is given at the start of that section. You will have a total of 45 minutes to complete the timed sections of the test.

7. Each section includes examples showing you how to answer the questions. You may refer to these examples at any time as you work through the section.

8. Do as many questions as you can. For some questions you will be given a range of options — if you get stuck on one of these questions, choose the answer that you think is most likely to be correct, then move on to the next question. If you get stuck on a question for which no options are given, leave it and move on to the next question. If you have time at the end of the section, go back and have another go at the questions you could not answer.

9. You should do any rough working on a separate piece of paper.

Work carefully, but go as quickly as you can.

Example | Read these example questions. You may return to these examples at any time as you work through this section.

HMS Iolaire — A Tragedy Follows a Victory

1   World War I had just ended, the Armistice had been agreed, and a large number of sailors were making their way home to Stornoway on the island of Lewis, off the west coast of Scotland. They were looking forward to coming home.

    However, in the early hours of January 1st, 1919, disaster struck. HMS Iolaire crashed

5   into the notorious 'Beasts of Holm', a set of rocks just a mile away from the safety of Stornoway harbour. Around 50 men jumped overboard, planning to swim the short distance to the shore. Sadly, the stormy seas and windy conditions meant that these men perished. Meanwhile, there were many fatalities on board as the ship began to sink. The alarm was raised and the town's coastguard was called out, but by the time he and his team arrived at

10   the scene of the disaster, the ship had sunk.

(A)   Why did the sailors have to travel to Stornoway by boat?

☐ **A**   Because Stornoway is on the west coast of Scotland
☐ **B**   Because they were on their way back from World War I
▬ **C**   Because Stornoway is on an island
☐ **D**   Because the 'Beasts of Holm' were dangerous

(B)   The 'Beasts of Holm' are described as "notorious" (line 5). What is meant by this?

☐ **A**   The rocks were concealed from view.
▬ **B**   The rocks were well known for being dangerous.
☐ **C**   Many people admired the rocks.
☐ **D**   The rocks had a mysterious reputation.

End of example questions

⚠ **Wait until you are told to go on** ⚠

There are 20 questions in this section

Read the passage carefully and then answer the questions that follow.

The Voyage of Ferdinand Magellan

1 **A Round World**

   With modern technology such as aeroplanes, satellites and space stations, there is now a lot of evidence that shows us that the world is round. However, this fact hasn't always been so easy to prove. Throughout history, many people believed that the world was flat.

5 The Greek philosopher Aristotle is thought to be one of the first people to suggest the idea that the world is round, doing so in around 350 BC. He looked at the sky and observed that it was possible to see different constellations depending on where you were in the world. This caused him to start wondering if the surface of the world could be curved.

   However, it was not until nearly two thousand years later that Aristotle's theory could

10 actually be proved. Without a way of viewing the world from above, this could only be done by travelling all the way around the world to finish in the same place you started from. Nobody was able to achieve this until the 16th century, when a Portuguese explorer called Ferdinand Magellan set off on a voyage that led to the first circumnavigation* of the globe.

The Story of Ferdinand Magellan

15   Ferdinand Magellan was born in Portugal in around 1480. During his lifetime, many Europeans were exploring the world and travelling to new places. Explorers would then update maps to show the new places they had been to. As a young man, Magellan travelled on expeditions to many places, including India and Africa. Many Europeans also travelled to a group of islands in South East Asia called the Spice Islands, which are now

20 known as the Maluku Islands. At this time, exotic spices like nutmeg and cloves were considered very valuable in Europe because they could only be found in faraway places that were expensive and dangerous to travel to.

   When Europeans first travelled to the Spice Islands, they sailed east to get there. However, Magellan believed that it might be quicker and easier to get to the islands by

25 sailing west instead. At first, Magellan tried to persuade the King of Portugal to pay for a westward voyage to the Spice Islands, but the King was unwilling to support such an expedition. Determined, Magellan moved from Portugal to Spain and convinced the King of Spain to fund the expedition instead. On September 20th 1519, the expedition left Spain with five ships and around 270 men.

Passage continues over the page ⟹

30 Reaching the other side of the Americas

The first part of Magellan's voyage involved crossing the Atlantic Ocean to reach South America. It had been less than 30 years since European explorers had discovered the Americas, and the ocean on the other side of the continent had never been reached by boats sailing from Europe. Upon reaching South America, Magellan's first challenge was to 35 find a way to reach the ocean on the other side. He believed there may be a route near the southern point of the continent that would save him from having to sail all the way around it. Eventually, the explorers found a sea channel that linked the Atlantic Ocean on the east side of the Americas to the ocean on the west.

However, the journey to this point had been far from smooth sailing. Before the ships even 40 reached the sea channel, Magellan had to put an end to a mutiny led by sailors who did not trust his leadership. The expedition also lost two of its five ships before they reached the other side of the Americas — one became shipwrecked, and another deserted the expedition and returned to Spain. When Magellan and his men finally arrived at the ocean on the other side, Magellan gave it the name that is still used today — the Pacific Ocean — meaning 45 'Peaceful Sea'. The channel they used was later named the Strait** of Magellan in his honour.

The End of the Voyage

The journey across the Pacific Ocean brought more danger to the expedition. Magellan had expected to cross the ocean quickly, but the journey actually took over three months The crew had to deal with dwindling supplies and extreme hunger. The expedition finally reached 50 land, arriving in South-East Asia in March 1521, but this did not mean an end to the difficulties faced by Magellan and his men. Around a month later, whilst visiting some islands in the Philippines, Magellan became involved in a conflict between two local tribal leaders and was killed in a battle, meaning that he never made it to the Spice Islands.

The expedition had to persevere without him, and the remainder of his crew reached the 55 Spice Islands several months later. Tragically, only one of the five ships made it back to Spain on September 8th 1522, carrying just 18 men. The small number of men who survived the perilous journey completed the first recorded circumnavigation of the world. Centuries after the Ancient Greeks walked the earth, Magellan's expedition finally proved Aristotle's theory that the world is round to be correct.

* circumnavigation — the act of travelling all the way around something
** strait — a thin channel of water that connects two seas

Answer these questions about the text. You can refer back to the text if you need to.
Pick the best answer and draw a line through the rectangle next to it.

(1) According to the text, why did Aristotle think that the world was round?

- [ ] **A** He saw that the moon and the sun were both round.
- [ ] **B** He went on an expedition from Greece to America.
- [ ] **C** He saw that different groups of stars were visible in different parts of the world.
- [ ] **D** He had been taught to believe the world was round.

(2) When Aristotle first suggested that the world was round, it was difficult to prove.
This is because:

- [ ] **A** nobody had invented boats.
- [ ] **B** no maps of the world had been drawn yet.
- [ ] **C** there was no way of viewing the world from above.
- [ ] **D** everyone was convinced that the world was flat.

(3) Where are the Spice Islands?

- [ ] **A** Spain
- [ ] **B** South America
- [ ] **C** South East Asia
- [ ] **D** Africa

(4) According to the text, why were spices such as nutmeg and cloves considered valuable in Europe during Magellan's lifetime?

- [ ] **A** They were not used much in European cooking.
- [ ] **B** Europeans wanted to trade them in Africa.
- [ ] **C** They added flavour to a range of dishes.
- [ ] **D** They were rare and hard to get.

(5) What was the purpose of Magellan's voyage?

- [ ] **A** To discover new lands
- [ ] **B** To find a western route to the Spice Islands
- [ ] **C** To be the first European to ever reach the Spice Islands
- [ ] **D** To reach the Pacific Ocean

Go to the next question ⇨

6 According to the text, which of the following statements about Ferdinand Magellan must be true?

- [ ] **A** He was born in the 4th century.
- [ ] **B** He travelled to India five times.
- [ ] **C** He left Portugal and relocated to Spain.
- [ ] **D** He began travelling when he was just eighteen years old.

7 Who paid for Magellan's voyage?

- [ ] **A** Magellan himself
- [ ] **B** The King of Portugal
- [ ] **C** The King of Spain
- [ ] **D** The Portuguese navy

8 According to the text, which of the following statements is false?

- [ ] **A** The Pacific Ocean is on the west side of the Americas.
- [ ] **B** The expedition crossed the Atlantic Ocean before the Pacific Ocean.
- [ ] **C** Europeans had already been to the Americas before Magellan arrived.
- [ ] **D** The expedition had to sail all the way around the tip of South America.

9 The journey to South America is described as being "far from smooth sailing" (line 39). This suggests that:

- [ ] **A** the journey went smoothly.
- [ ] **B** the sailors travelled a great distance.
- [ ] **C** the sailors were unprepared.
- [ ] **D** the journey was eventful.

10 How many of Magellan's ships made it through the sea channel to the Pacific Ocean?

- [ ] **A** Two
- [ ] **B** Three
- [ ] **C** Four
- [ ] **D** Five

11 Which of the following was named by Magellan?

    ☐ **A**   The Atlantic Ocean
    ☐ **B**   The Pacific Ocean
    ☐ **C**   The Strait of Magellan
    ☐ **D**   South America

12 Which of the following difficulties did the expedition not face?

    ☐ **A**   Extreme hunger
    ☐ **B**   Mutinies
    ☐ **C**   Attacks from pirates
    ☐ **D**   Supplies running low

13 Reaching land "did not mean an end to the difficulties faced by Magellan and his men" (lines 50-51). This suggests that:

    ☐ **A**   Magellan and his men were never able to reach land.
    ☐ **B**   Magellan and his men encountered more problems after they reached land.
    ☐ **C**   Magellan and his men were safe while at sea, but in danger on the land.
    ☐ **D**   Magellan and his men experienced no more problems after reaching land.

14 Which of the following best describes Ferdinand Magellan?

    ☐ **A**   The first person to suggest that the world was round
    ☐ **B**   The first person to lead a European voyage across the Pacific Ocean
    ☐ **C**   The first Spanish person to circumnavigate the globe
    ☐ **D**   The first person to discover the Spice Islands

15 In which year did Magellan die?

    ☐ **A**   1519
    ☐ **B**   1520
    ☐ **C**   1521
    ☐ **D**   1522

Go to the next question ⇨

(16) Which of the following statements about Magellan's westward voyage is true?

☐ **A** Magellan made it as far as the Spice Islands.
☐ **B** The journey took less than four years.
☐ **C** There were not enough men left to sail back to Spain.
☐ **D** The sailors returned from the Spice Islands the same way they had come.

(17) What does the word "exotic" mean (line 20)?

☐ **A** Delicious
☐ **B** Colourful
☐ **C** Unusual
☐ **D** Expensive

(18) What does the phrase "Magellan had to put an end to a mutiny" mean (line 40)?

☐ **A** He had to prevent his ship from crashing.
☐ **B** He had to stop an uprising.
☐ **C** He had to fight off an attack from a rival ship.
☐ **D** He had to cancel a part of the expedition.

(19) What does the word "persevere" mean (line 54)?

☐ **A** Continue
☐ **B** Navigate
☐ **C** Regroup
☐ **D** Conclude

(20) What does the word "perilous" mean (line 57)?

☐ **A** Expensive
☐ **B** Disorganised
☐ **C** Illegal
☐ **D** Dangerous

⊗ Stop — you may check your answers in this section only

BLANK PAGE

9

© CGP 2019

Example Read this example question. You may return to this example at any time as you work through this section.

Rearrange the words so that each sentence makes sense.
Mark the rectangle under the word which does **not** fit into the sentence.

A it for time was late bed
▢ ▢ ▢ ▢ ▬ ▢

The remaining words can be rearranged to make the sentence: 'It was time for bed.'

⚠ **Wait until you are told to go on** ⚠

🕕 **You have 6 minutes to complete this section** 🕕

There are 15 questions in this section

Rearrange the words so that each sentence makes sense.
Mark the rectangle under the word which does **not** fit into the sentence.

1 scissors cut when run don't holding you're
▢ ▢ ▢ ▢ ▢ ▢ ▢

2 by the is island swam only boat accessible
▢ ▢ ▢ ▢ ▢ ▢ ▢ ▢

3 piano day the many practise you every should
▢ ▢ ▢ ▢ ▢ ▢ ▢ ▢

4 tree of the jumped the squirrel climb out
▢ ▢ ▢ ▢ ▢ ▢ ▢ ▢

5 hates smelling eggs of Julie rotten taste the
▢ ▢ ▢ ▢ ▢ ▢ ▢ ▢

6 health fruit enough children eat vegetables and the don't
▢ ▢ ▢ ▢ ▢ ▢ ▢ ▢ ▢

7   gloves   birthday   a   for   hat   my   got   new   I
□   □   □ □ □ □ □   □   □

8   shining   happy   he   heat   when   feels   the   always   is   sun
□   □   □   □   □   □   □   □   □   □

9   on   a   story   read   night   Priya   write   Sunday   short
□ □   □   □   □   □   □   □   □

10   could   raining   Dima   distance   hear   in   rumbling   the   thunder
□   □   □   □   □   □   □   □   □

11   was   everyone   there   were   friendly   met   really   we
□   □   □   □   □   □   □   □

12   picture   a   green   drew   a   Tom   dinosaur   of   photograph
□   □   □   □   □   □   □   □   □

13   a   France   me   postcard   you   when   send   to   holiday   get
□   □   □   □   □   □   □   □   □   □

14   right   in   biscuits   are   left   jar   the   no   there
□   □   □   □   □   □   □   □   □

15   roundabout   father   illness   in   near   my   the   works   the   hospital
□   □   □   □   □   □   □   □   □   □

Stop — you may check your answers in this section only

Example Read this example question. You may return to this example at any time as you work through this section.

Choose the word which means the same, or nearly the same, as the word on the left.

A **small** tiny strong large soft
▬ ☐ ☐ ☐

⚠ **Wait until you are told to go on** ⚠

(7) **You have 7 minutes to complete this section** (7)

There are 20 questions in this section

Choose the word which means the same, or nearly the same, as the word on the left.

(1) **expand** restrict grow pull advance
☐ ☐ ☐ ☐

(2) **reign** rule leader follow government
☐ ☐ ☐ ☐

(3) **decent** humble spiritual proper wise
☐ ☐ ☐ ☐

(4) **comfortable** idle cosy awkward satisfactory
☐ ☐ ☐ ☐

(5) **frightened** cowardly ghastly stunned petrified
☐ ☐ ☐ ☐

(6) **available** present free potential used
☐ ☐ ☐ ☐

(7) **visible** seeing noticeable invisible loud
☐ ☐ ☐ ☐

(8) **mischievous** destructive threatening clumsy naughty
☐ ☐ ☐ ☐

9 **chance**

expectation ▭ freedom ▭ relief ▭ opportunity ▭

10 **profession**

employee ▭ qualification ▭ job ▭ specialist ▭

11 **continuous**

unbroken ▭ connected ▭ lengthy ▭ uncertain ▭

12 **flaw**

benefit ▭ blame ▭ fault ▭ calamity ▭

13 **hero**

person ▭ character ▭ celebrity ▭ idol ▭

14 **produce**

multiply ▭ generate ▭ prepare ▭ design ▭

15 **offend**

disturb ▭ insult ▭ mourn ▭ distract ▭

16 **rational**

educated ▭ logical ▭ original ▭ pessimistic ▭

17 **trade**

exchange ▭ give ▭ purchase ▭ auction ▭

18 **luxurious**

rare ▭ extravagant ▭ unbelievable ▭ mature ▭

19 **analyse**

break ▭ think ▭ examine ▭ notice ▭

20 **effect**

consequence ▭ reason ▭ attraction ▭ aim ▭

✖ Stop — you may check your answers in this section only

Section 4: Verbal Reasoning — Cloze

Example **Read these example questions. You may return to these examples at any time as you work through this section.**

A The Solar System is made up of [p][l][a][n][e][t][s], asteroids and other

B bodies orbiting the Sun. Earth is the [t][h][i][r][d] planet from the Sun,

C after Mercury and [V][e][n][u][s].

⚠ Wait until you are told to go on ⚠

⏱ You have 8 minutes to complete this section ⏱

There are 22 questions in this section

1 King Arthur is one of the most [ ][a][ ][ ][u][s] characters in British mythology.

2 [ ][l][t][ ][ ][u][ ][h] it is likely that a ruler called Arthur really did exist most

3 of the stories about him are completely [f][ ][ ][t][ ][ ][n][a][l]. The first

4 [r][e][ ][o][ ][ ][e][d] mention of Arthur comes from the work of Nennius, a

ninth-century monk. However, most of the tales that are well-known today come

5 from a collection [ ][ ][i][t][ ][e][n] in around 1470 by Thomas Malory,

6 a nobleman and criminal who wrote his manuscript from [p][ ][i][s][ ][ ].

7 One of the most commonly retold tales [ ][e][s][ ][r][ ][b][ ][s] how

Arthur became king. As he was raised by a knight called Sir Ector, Arthur didn't

8 know that he was the son of the previous king and the rightful [h][ ][ ][r] to the

throne since the king had passed away. When Arthur grew up, the wizard Merlin

9 placed a sword called Excalibur into a stone and d[ ][ ]l a[ ]e d that

whoever could remove the sword would be the true king. Arthur was the only person

10 to successfully remove the sword and so p[ ]o[ ][ ]d his right to the throne.

11 A[ ][ ]o r[ ]i n[ ] to legend, King Arthur lived in a great castle

12 called Camelot. Some people b[ ][ ]l[ ][ ]v e that Tintagel Castle in

Cornwall may even be the same castle as the legendary Camelot. It is at Camelot

13 that Arthur kept his Round Table, which was d[ ][ ][ ]g[ ]e d so that each

knight sitting at it would be viewed as an equal.

14 Arthur's most l[ ][ ]a l knight and greatest friend was Sir Lancelot.

15 Lancelot and his son famously set out on a [ ]u[ ]s t for the Holy Grail — an

enchanted cup that supposedly had the power to heal wounds and grant eternal

16 youth. [ ]e[ ]p[ ]t e his friendship with Arthur, Lancelot was fated to fall

17 in love with Arthur's wife, Guinevere. Their f o[ ][ ]i d[ ]e n romance

18 sparked a chain of events that [ ][ ]o u[ ]h t about Arthur's downfall.

19 Many books, poems and films have been [ ]a[ ]e d on the various

tales of King Arthur and his Knights of the Round Table, making him one of the most

20 [ ]e[ ]o[ ]n i[ ]a b l e characters in the Western world.

21 However, the h[ ][ ]t o[ ][ ]c a l facts suggest that the modern-day

22 [ ]m[ ]g[ ] of Arthur as a glorious king with a magic sword is very different

to what the real Arthur might have looked like.

❌ **Stop — you may check your answers in this section only**

Example Read these example questions. You may return to these examples at any time as you work through this section.

A Work out which 3D figure has been rotated to make the new 3D figure.

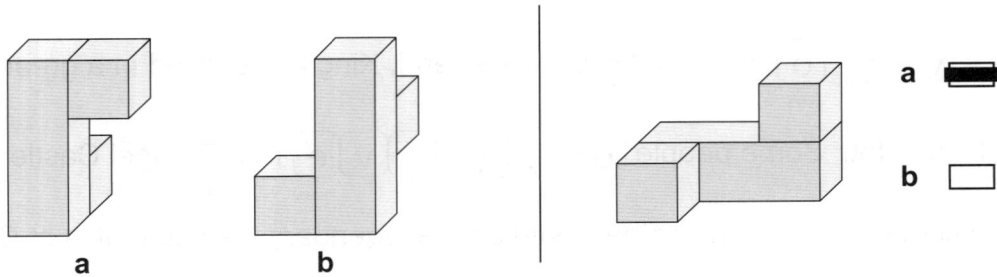

a

b

a ▬

b ▢

B Work out which option is a top-down 2D view of the 3D figure on the left.

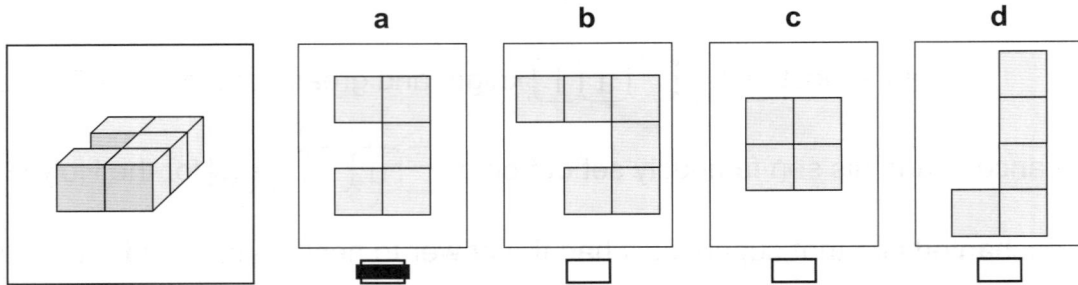

a   b   c   d

▬   ▢   ▢   ▢

C A square is folded and then a hole is punched, as shown on the left. Work out which option shows the square when unfolded.

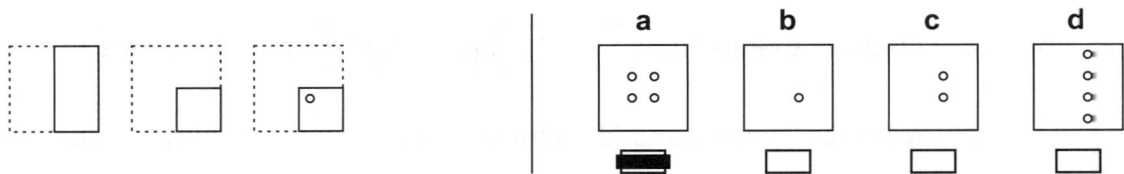

a   b   c   d

▬   ▢   ▢   ▢

D Work out which of the four cubes can be made from the net.

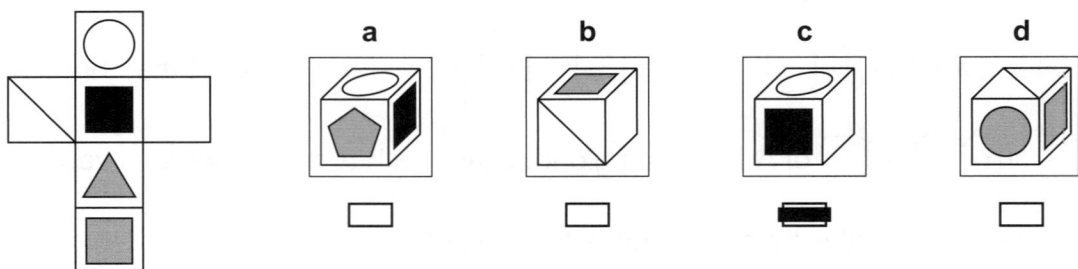

a   b   c   d

▢   ▢   ▬   ▢

⚠ **Wait until you are told to go on** ⚠

There are 18 questions in this section

Work out which 3D figure has been rotated to make the new 3D figure.

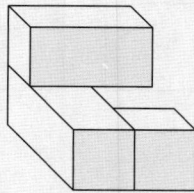
a

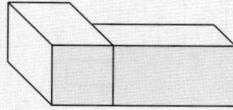
c

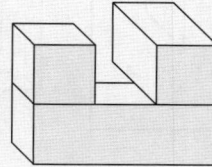
e

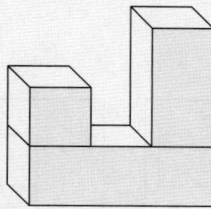
b

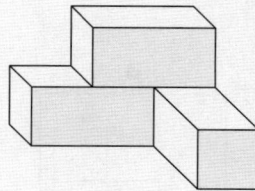
d

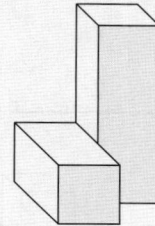
f

①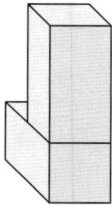

a ☐   d ☐

b ☐   e ☐

c ☐   f ☐

②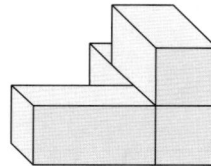

a ☐   d ☐

b ☐   e ☐

c ☐   f ☐

③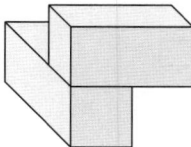

a ☐   d ☐

b ☐   e ☐

c ☐   f ☐

④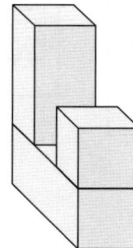

a ☐   d ☐

b ☐   e ☐

c ☐   f ☐

⑤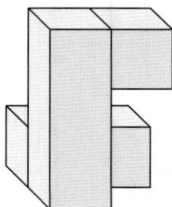

a ☐   d ☐

b ☐   e ☐

c ☐   f ☐

⑥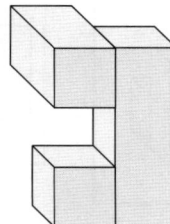

a ☐   d ☐

b ☐   e ☐

c ☐   f ☐

Go to the next question ⇨

Work out which option is a top-down 2D view of the 3D figure on the left.

7 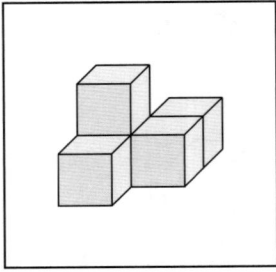   **a** 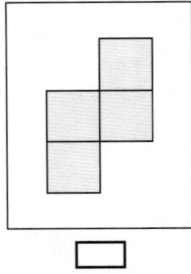   **b** 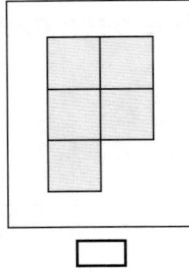   **c** 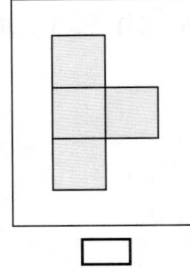   **d**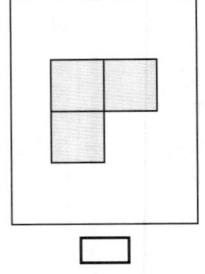

8 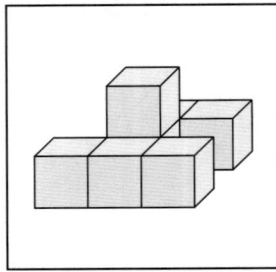   **a** 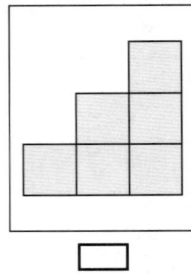   **b** 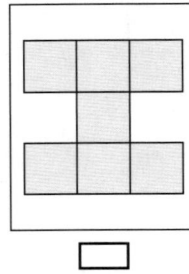   **c** 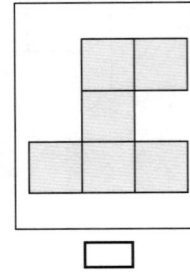   **d**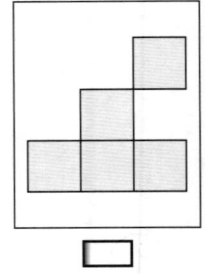

9 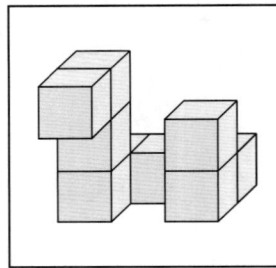   **a** 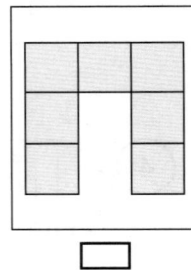   **b** 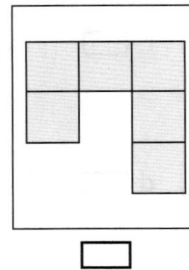   **c** 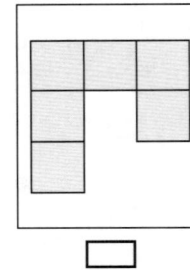   **d**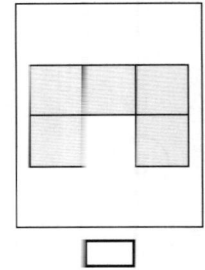

10 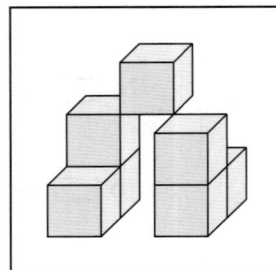   **a** 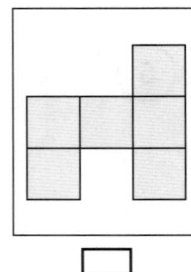   **b** 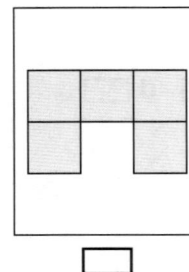   **c** 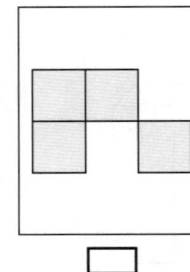   **d**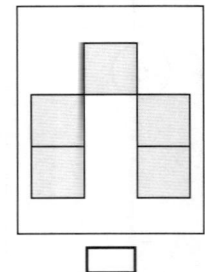

A square is folded and then a hole is punched, as shown on the left.
Work out which option shows the square when unfolded.

11

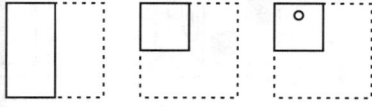

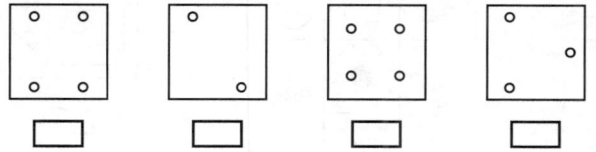

12

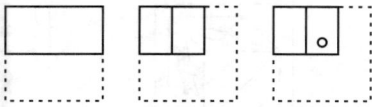

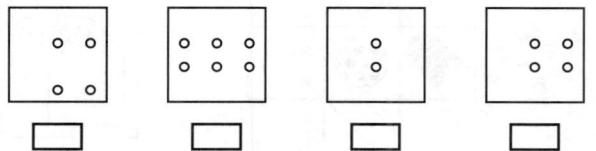

13

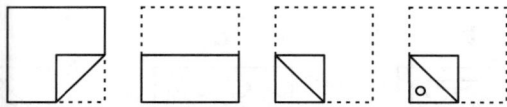

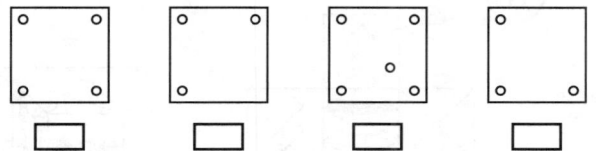

14

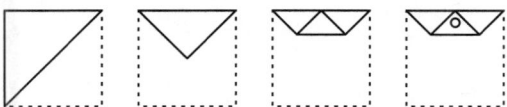

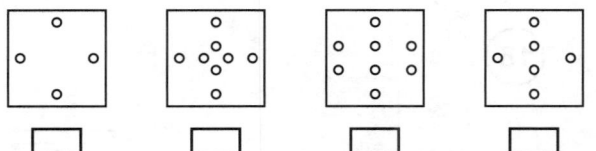

Go to the next question ⟹

Work out which of the four cubes can be made from the net.

(15)

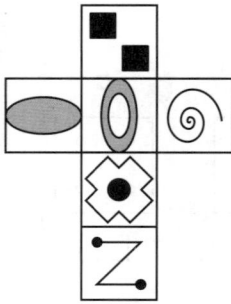

a
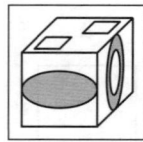
☐

b
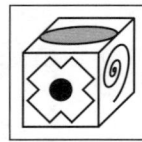
☐

c
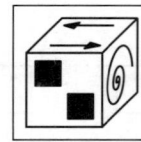
☐

d

☐

(16)

a

☐

b

☐

c

☐

d

☐

(17)

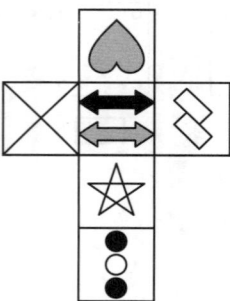

a
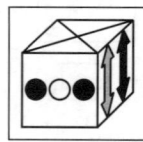
☐

b
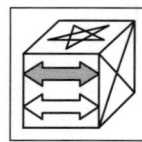
☐

c
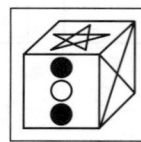
☐

d

☐

(18)

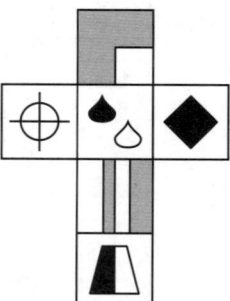

a

☐

b
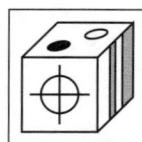
☐

c
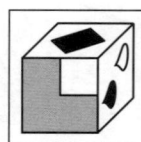
☐

d

☐

⊗ **Stop — you may check your answers in this section only**